C000078283

OLD WORLD
NEW WORLD
AND THE
REAL WORLD

OLD WORLD
NEW WORLD
AND THE
REAL WORLD

HOW TO GROW YOUR BUSINESS IN HALF THE TIME

JOHN STEIN

TWF Publications

This edition published in Great Britain by
TWF Publications
Goss Chambers
Goss Street
Chester, CH1 2BG
Tel: 01244 401401

British Library Cataloguing-in-Publication Data
A catalogue record for this book is available from the British Library

ISBN 0 9547134 0 0

Designed and typeset by Home Communications Ltd, Manchester
Printed in Great Britain by Masons Print Group, Chester

To Linda

CONTENTS

FOREWORD

One of the most challenging aspects of being a consultant is to deliver a message to an audience at an event or conference in a manner in which they will remember it long after they have gone their separate ways. The same principle, I'm told, applies to writing.

To this end, I needed a theme that would reflect my approach to business growth and success. The pyramid concept was chosen as there is a real similarity between this symbol of endurance, power and strength and the requirements of businesses in today's world. Further research and development of the concept would end in the writing of 'The Real World'.

The pyramid is probably the best example of ancient precision engineering known today. Simple but impressive, the structure comprises a square base as its foundation, four sloping sides and a cap pointing towards the heavens.

As a design icon, the pyramid shape is perceived by many as elegant and timeless; indeed, many modern buildings, including hotels, casinos, art galleries and even homes, have taken inspiration from the original Egyptian pyramid.

I've met many people over the years that have marvelled at the work of the Ancient Egyptians. Perhaps holidays have allowed them to see the pyramids first hand, or they have used the imagery to decorate their homes. Ancient Egyptian culture also influences many parts of our life today, from food and jewellery and even the clothes we wear. People can identify and connect with many things Egyptian.

More importantly to the writing of 'The Real World', in Egypt today eighty such structures still exist. They have truly stood the test of time. That in itself is an impressive feat.

The Great Pyramid at Giza, built for King Khufi in c.2589 BC, is the only survivor of the seven wonders of the ancient world and is the largest pyramid of any created by the Egyptian Pharaohs. It is still the largest stone structure ever built. At 450 ft tall (138m), the Great Pyramid dwarfs the Arc de Triumphe by nearly 300 ft, is 150ft taller than New York's Statue of Liberty and would tower over St Paul's Cathedral by some 90 ft.

In order to tell 'The Real World' story, some additional background information linked to the building of the pyramids might be of help.

THE OLD WORLD AND THE NEW WORLD

In Ancient Egypt the Pharaohs ruled supreme. They were, for the most part, loved by their people and, in return, provided for them in every way they could. The Pharaoh was believed to be both a genius and a god and as a result was worshipped, feared and respected by his people, both in life and in death. The Pharaohs enjoyed a lavish lifestyle and, not surprisingly, wanted this to continue long after death. To this end, they spent a considerable amount of wealth, time and energy preparing for death. Part of this preparation involved the building of the pyramid.

The pyramid was built primarily as the perfect final resting-place for the deceased Pharaoh and to help transfer him (or her, as there were several female Pharaohs) on the journey to the next world. The people called this 'the Afterlife' and it was every Egyptian's duty to guarantee the Pharaoh's passage from the Old World into the New World by helping, if requested, in the construction.

An architect was commissioned to design and oversee the building of the Pharaoh's Pyramid. As you might expect over hundreds of years of pyramid building, experience and knowledge was handed down through generations. Plans were never publicly produced, with the secrets of building the pyramid known only to a few.

The architect's main challenge was to constantly innovate and try to build the impossible. Expectations were always high. Each Pharaoh was ambitious and demanding and required a unique creative twist to his completed monument, which would differentiate his pyramid from those built before.

Building the pyramid was a massive undertaking, involving thousands of people from around the kingdom. The Egyptian subjects were happy to work on the project, as they believed the pyramid would immortalise their king and would ultimately bring them good fortune when it was their time to pass to the New World. Some people devoted their whole life to the building of the monument.

DISPELLING A FEW MYTHS

The pyramids, despite the popular misconception to the contrary, were not built by slaves but by highly skilled craftsmen including masons, carpenters, plasterers and painters. Egyptians believed in the pursuit of excellence and were very proud of the quality of their work.

Again, in contrast to the images depicted by Hollywood filmmakers over the years, a slave system did not exist in Egypt. A form of national service prevailed throughout the kingdom and it was viewed as an honour to work on behalf of the Pharaoh.

In matters of Egyptian law, women enjoyed an equal status with men. They were allowed to own or rent property, conduct a business, divorce and remarry. They could also reign as Pharaoh, as Cleopatra did before Egypt came under the control of Imperial Rome. Its worth noting that the women of Egypt played as important a role as the men in supporting the Pharaoh's vision.

Finally there is a common belief that pyramids were built only for

Pharaohs. This is also a myth. Pyramids were also built for other members of Egyptian society and at one time became a regular and permanent part of the landscape of Egypt.

THE REAL WORLD

Learning more about the mystique behind the pyramids enabled me to realise that, in many instances, there was a direct correlation between the 'Pyramid Building Journey' of the Pharaoh and the 'Business Growth Journey' of the business leader.

To begin with, the Pharaoh and the business leader share a common, single-minded determination to create something totally unique.

In the case of the Pharaoh, it was to build a monument that could not only transfer him to the New World but which would also benefit all of his people. Long after he had gone, his pyramid would be recognised as a dynamic place to visit, to relax with others and somewhere to worship. The pyramid would be designed for the living as well as the dead. Pyramids were for everyone, whatever their status in Egyptian society. People would proudly say 'we built that'.

In the case of forward thinking business leaders today, the desire is to build a solid and successful organisation, which differentiates clearly from others in their chosen marketplace. They often wish to create a truly outstanding business, where above-average growth becomes the norm for the organisation. Like the pyramid, the organisation is designed for the living and to enable people to also say 'we built that'.

You can, perhaps, understand why the linking of ancient Egypt and the 'The Real World' of commerce seemed a good idea.

To support this thinking I also noted the following.

The pyramid building 'journey' towards completion involved six key phases. My Winning [formula]™ approach to the business growth 'journey' also involves six key stages. This forms the core of 'The Real World' story.

Both journeys involve the initial development of a vision by a single person. In the Egyptian kingdom this was the Pharaoh's responsibility and in the commercial world of today it is the business leader's – the Chief Executive, Managing Director, Owner Manager or Entrepreneur. Leadership plays a critical role in the development, support to and realisation of any vision, whether you are a Pharaoh or a Chief Executive.

Similarities also exist in the period involved on the journey of the Pharaoh and the Egyptian people and the journey faced by the business leader and the people within the organisation.

In the time in which our story is set, building a pyramid could take up to 20 years, whilst today most business growth journeys take between 3 and 5 years.

Although the story is based in ancient Egypt, the highs and lows experienced in business today could easily echo the events, experiences and outcomes involved in the building of the pyramid over four thousand years ago. This again, forms a major part of 'The Real World' story.

Leading people into the unknown was then, and is often the case today, an important but unexpected part of the journey. For example, very few Egyptian people had previous experience of building a pyramid. It could take twenty years to build the pyramid and the workforce would constantly change over the lifespan of the construction.

Similarly, very few business leaders have experience and knowledge in the unique dynamics of growing a business. It's quite common for them to readily admit that they are experiencing the growth journey themselves for the first time.

Building the pyramid therefore involved asking people to take a leap of faith in the possible, to trust the leader (the Pharaoh), his officials and the journey. This principle often applies today to the workforce connected to an organisation with new, ambitious and exciting plans for growth. They are often asked to trust the business leaders.

'THE REAL WORLD' STORY

Using the link with Ancient Egypt and the Winning [formula]™ approach to business growth, 'The Real World' story unravels the mystique around the 'journey' and in a simple way describes in detail the various stages that you will encounter along the way in your organisation.

INTRODUCTION

EVERYONE DREAMS OF BEING PART OF A SUCCESSFUL BUSINESS

Every Entrepreneur, Chief Executive Officer, Senior Vice President, Managing Director and Owner Manager I have ever met dreams of building a successful and growing organisation. As business leaders they rarely consider the prospect of failure.

Likewise, employees dream of being part of a successful and growing organisation. No one nowadays wants to work for, or be part of, a failing business.

Success and growth are the biggest discussion areas in any boardroom, in any company, anywhere on the planet. In today's highly competitive world, the cost of failure is high, but the benefits associated with success can change people's lives.

A successful and growing business benefits everyone at every level in the organisation

- Job security is achieved offering peace of mind to many
- Career opportunities become available for those who want them
- New skills can be learnt as people are personally developed
- Friendships are often formed that can last a lifetime
- Salary and wage increases can be obtained
- Bonuses are often available as part of the company's reward programme

Very few people, however, realise the dream or benefit from being part of this unique business experience. In a work life of, say, thirty years, they will be lucky to personally enjoy two or three truly motivating and worthwhile job experiences. Very few will also be lucky to be part of a growing and successful organisation, even once in their lifetime. If you have beaten these odds, then congratulate yourself. If you are currently experiencing the joys of success and growth be thankful. Many of your friends have not, or will not, beat these odds.

DREAMING OF SUCCESS ISN'T ENOUGH

The growth journey is surprising to some people, challenging to many and rewarding to everyone. It is a dynamic and demanding process, giving people the opportunity to explore new possibilities that can help them achieve their full potential, whatever that may be.

It's often viewed by ambitious business leaders as a never-ending journey. Success and growth feed a need for more success, and more growth.

But dreaming of success isn't enough. Growth is hard to achieve. It also gets tougher to achieve each year. It involves a strong work ethic as you and your colleagues manoeuvre the many twists and turns on the journey.

CHALLENGES FACING A GROWING ORGANISATION

Your organisation will be faced with many challenges, each one designed to test you at strategic and operational levels and off course, at a personal level.

Some of the challenges may include:

- Customer retention
- Sustaining and maintaining sales and revenue streams
- Improving productivity and efficiency throughout the business

- Managing your organisation's growth and the expected change required to ensure it happens
- Sustaining employee focus on your plans for growth and success
- Further development of your recruitment and selection process
- Integration of new products and services into your marketplace
- Development of your overall growth strategy
- Handling of any proposed acquisitions in the future
- Development and marketing of your brand
- Activity linked to out-performing the competition in your marketplace
- Retention of existing personnel throughout the company
- Funding and investment support required to grow
- The use of IT, including the development of new infrastructures and systems
- Motivation of employees throughout the organisation
- Communication at all levels throughout the organisation
- Training, education and development of your people
- Delivery of agreed customer service levels
- Differentiation between your organisation and others in your marketplace
- Gaining widespread support for the evolution of your company

You can see from the list why many business leaders view the journey as never ending.

THE WINNING [FORMULA]™

The Winning [formula]™ approach highlighted in 'The Real World' will enable you to meet these challenges. It will demonstrate the part that each person can play in your organisation's future success. Applying the Winning [formula] ™ will also ensure that more people take responsibility for their own, and your organisation's, growth and success in the future.

The approach is unique, simple, tried, tested and proven to work. The development process began in 1992 and, since then, with the support of clients, has produced spectacular results for their businesses. Their input, feedback and results over the years have helped produce a model that demystifies growth and success in such a way that people are no longer confused by the term 'strategy'. I am immensely proud of the outstanding results achieved by my clients, and of the difference these results have made to the quality of life of the people connected with each organisation.

The approach has been used to accelerate expansion plans, support new investment, launch management buy outs, change the direction of long standing businesses and support plans by newly appointed Chief Executives, Senior Vice Presidents and Managing Directors. Entrepreneurs have also used it to support the purchase or launch of new business ventures.

THE REAL WORLD

The methods highlighted in 'The Real World' are also linked to the reality of the real world, in which we live and work. Sound theory has been supported by a pragmatic approach to meeting the needs of our client business leaders. How often have you heard a manager say 'welcome to the real world' or, 'we're not in the real world' or even worse 'get real'? The 'Real World' has almost become the business catchphrase of our time.

In their defence, the need to acknowledge the real world is based on the demands of our time. Speed of response is critical in virtually every business sector. Technology has changed our world forever. There doesn't seem to be enough hours in any day. Long-term strategic planning is often supplemented by the need for short-term success and the achievement of 'quick wins'.

The Winning [formula]™ approach in 'The Real World' is based in the real world, and is about your business, in the real world. Each component part of the Winning [formula]™ works.

'The Real World' will show you how to:
- Increase you and your colleagues' understanding of the growth process
- Produce a blueprint for success to use on your journey
- Enlist support from your people to your ambitious plans
- Overcome the challenges you will face in the future
- Change the people mindset in your organisation
- Create a culture of outstanding performance
- Improve motivation and communication within your organisation
- Energise your people to meet new targets and goals
- Maximise the talent which exists within your business
- Sustain support for your plans for growth

More importantly 'The Real World' will demonstrate to you
HOW TO GROW YOUR BUSINESS IN HALF THE TIME.

'The Real World' is for anyone connected with an ambitious organisation, whether you are an employee, stakeholder or supplier. It highlights what it could be like on the journey and also the personal contribution expected to ensure future and long lasting success.

One of the most energising journeys any person can experience is the business growth journey. Good luck and safe passage, wherever it may take you.

John Stein
Mauritius, November 2003

ADVICE TO A PHARAOH

The Pharaoh had been ill for several months and knew that she would soon make her next and final journey, from life to death. The sun god Osiris was, she hoped, ready to receive her.

She had ruled the kingdom of Egypt for over twenty-five years and in that period had maintained its position as the wealthiest country in the world. She had also enjoyed many years of peace and harmony with Egypt's neighbours, Syria and Nubia.

The people loved their queen and she had served them well. The harvests had been good, food was plentiful, trade with other countries flourished and the people were healthy. All was well in the kingdom.

This was in considerable contrast to the kingdom she had inherited from her father, where mistrust, cynicism, selfishness and greed had prevailed. Her father had reigned for only seven years but, in that time, the damage to the country had been extensive. His style of leadership ensured that almost every part of Egyptian society was corrupt. The people had been deeply unhappy and the country was constantly at war with its neighbours.

Succession to the throne had entailed making dramatic changes to the way the country was ruled, but, with the growing support of the people, she had created a new optimistic and honest culture and Egyptians were, once again, proud to be Egyptian.

From the start of her reign she was an ambitious and demanding Pharaoh, one with a clear idea of what needed to change. This was combined with a rather low tolerance for those who did not support the royal policies. She was and had been firm and fair, but always true to her word.

Her vision for the new Egypt had entailed challenges. She had asked her people to conquer the unknown and believe in the possible. At first they didn't fully understand just what she meant but in time they came, not only to understand, but also to play their part in the country's golden era.

The same vigour and attention to detail that was a feature of her reign was still very evident as she prepared for death. Part of the planning process involved securing the future of her son - her husband was long dead - and the court that had so long supported her.

The most important element of her meticulous planning, which had begun almost as soon as she ascended the throne, involved the building of her pyramid, which had taken some sixteen years to complete.

The Royal Architect had designed a truly impressive monument and, such was its scale, that the stone steps on the structure's sides looked as if they were built into the sky. An enthusiastic workforce, happy to help the Pharaoh plan for her journey to the stars, had completed the pyramid ahead of schedule.

The Pyramid stood 280 feet high, encased in limestone that gleamed in the Egyptian sun. Within, secret passages were designed to fend off future tomb raiders, with false chambers to confuse them and granite doors to restrict entry to the Queen's Chamber. Finally, leading to that chamber, was the Grand Gallery that would be sealed when the Pharaoh was finally laid to rest.

It would be impossible to enter the Pyramid from the outside and, once inside, the Pharaoh could begin death's journey.

The final part of the Pharaoh's preparation involved a meeting with her son, the young prince, who would follow in his mother's footsteps and, on her death, be crowned Pharaoh in turn.

It is the role of all mothers, no matter what their status, to worry about their children. The prince, whose name was Smendes, was a fine young man but whether he was ready to rule was, at least to some, a matter of concern.

He wasn't actually disliked by the people but they often had to comfort themselves with the thought that at least he wasn't his grandfather. Boys, however, will be boys and Smendes was no different.

Chariots had become a passion with him and he would often be found racing through the streets surrounding the palace at speeds deemed by all to be unseemly and by many as downright dangerous.

Some things don't change.

It's not easy to discuss death with a parent, but the passage from this life to the next was of great importance to the Egyptians, and so the Queen and her son talked.

They considered the funeral and the young prince assured the Pharaoh that every one of the final arrangements would be attended to, whilst expressing his sincere hope that the time for these to be put in place would be many years hence.

They then moved on to matters of state. The Pharaoh began:

"You have learnt a great deal in my reign and I hope you are ready to receive the crown and the throne."

Smendes listened intently and, as he did so, began to realise with greater clarity than ever the full weight of his coming responsibilities.

Taking his mother's hand in his, he replied "I hope I can also achieve great things mother, and that you will be proud of me. I have learnt a great deal, but there seems such a lot to remember, to think about and to do. Where should I start?"

The Pharaoh remembered a similar but disappointing meeting she had with her own father and didn't want to miss this opportunity to help her son.

"It won't be easy, but there are three essential things you must do. If you carry them out, you will have a successful reign and a peaceful and harmonious life as the King.

"The first thing you will need to do is to look after your people and they, in turn, will look after the kingdom. You may soon be the ruler of Egypt, but without the support of your people you will never achieve great things."

The prince felt his mother was stating the obvious, but nodded in agreement.

"Secondly, begin the process of building your own pyramid as soon as you are able because the construction could take up most of your reign. The task will be fraught with challenges, frustrations and many difficulties but you must persist to ensure your own passage to the next world."

The young prince knew the truth of this. He had heard countless stories from scholars and scribes regarding past Pharaohs who failed to fulfil promises to their people.

He waited for the final piece of advice.

"In building the pyramid, you will need a strong and capable team of advisers, scholars and officials. You may have an idea of the personalities who will make up your team, but the best advice I can give you is to spend time with a man you will not yet have met.

"There lives in the land of Egypt a man known by some as the Sage, or the True Scholar. He is wise in many things and a loyal subject, although you may find him somewhat eccentric. Don't let this give the wrong impression for this is the man who, above all others, will help you.

"He holds the secrets to building the Pyramid. He has the formula. Talk to him my son."

The prince was confused. He thought the secrets lay with the architect and a select band of his men. Surely this True Scholar wasn't party to the secrets of the Pyramid, he thought.

"Why have I never heard of this man, mother?" asked Smendes.

"Because," replied the Pharaoh, "whilst I have consulted him privately on many occasions my father, your grandfather, had him banished from the court before I gained the throne."

"What was his crime?"

His mother smiled, as if at some private recollection.

"Something happened to your grandfather on the only occasion he visited the Sage's home and he never forgave him for it."

He wanted to ask his mother to tell him more about the Sage, but the Pharaoh was beginning to tire and, consequently, the prince thought he would question her further on the following day.

He kissed her goodnight. "I will see you tomorrow."

His mother looked at him. "Remember my advice," she whispered.

In the middle of the night the Pharaoh died. Smendes was woken to be given the news and handed a papyrus copy of his mother's final words, written by her physician.

The inscription read: *'Great is a great one whose great ones are great.'*

THE JOURNEY TO THE NEW WORLD

The meticulous planning carried out by the late Pharaoh, the prince and the court officials had made sure that her funeral was as she would have wished in every detail.

The Pharaoh's body began the journey from her palace, along the Nile on the Royal Barge. Thousands lined the banks, paying their last respects to a beloved queen.

Many of the mourners had played a personal part in the Pharaoh's final journey. They had helped in the construction of the magnificent barge, the Mortuary Temple and, of course, the Pyramid.

The journey up the Nile was slow and solemn, for it was important that every Egyptian had an opportunity to see for themselves the final journey of the dead Pharaoh.

The Royal Barge eventually reached the quayside, where the aromatic cedar coffin was carried up the causeway to the Mortuary Temple. At the same time, the barge was dismantled to be placed near to the Pharaoh in her chamber, where it could be used again in the afterlife.

The Pharaoh's coffin was taken into the Queen's Chamber within the pyramid and lowered into the Sarcophagus, surrounded by prized possessions, gifts to the gods and materials designed to support the success of her journey.

One of these caught the attention of the prince, as it seemed out of keeping with the array of luxurious items that his mother had chosen to accompany her on her last journey.

It was a life sized carving, in soapstone, of a tortoise; a tortoise with a particularly malicious expression on its small face.

The prince's new journey began with his return to the palace for a banquet celebrating the life of the deceased Pharaoh. After the banquet, he received each guest and personal condolences were offered.

The young prince took some comfort from these but, despite the planning and anticipation, his mind was still in turmoil. He had not only lost his beloved mother but now had to face the reality of taking over the rule of his kingdom.

There was, however, little time for such introspection as he was reminded by an official of his duty to thank his guests individually for their support. Greeting each guest would take some time and he didn't want to create a wrong impression. He knew that many of the people attending the banquet were already beginning to form opinions about him as the soon to be crowned Pharaoh.

He spent time with everyone, putting them at ease, listening intently to their offers of help and thanking them for attending.

At the end of the procession of guests was one man who was particularly eager to meet the Pharaoh to be. This was the person of whom his mother had spoken. The prince had noticed over dinner that he stood out from the other scholars and very rarely spoke, instead listening, nodding and smiling but not really engaging with people around him.

Now it seems to be a universal and ancient truth that persons of great intellect often display certain eccentricities, and this was no less true of the man the prince now studied.

He was exceptionally tall and, in contrast to the prevailing style of shaven heads for both men and women, his broad brow was topped by a mass of white hair that appeared to be on an independent journey towards the vaulted ceiling of the banqueting chamber.

He was dressed in a floor-length robe, obviously cut from fine cloth, but very simple in style. The contrast between this striking figure and the short, dark frame of the richly attired prince could not have been greater.

At last the two men met and the scholar bowed deeply before the prince, all the while fixing him with a knowing gaze.

"Your mother was a great woman, sir, she will be sadly missed," he said in a deep, slightly accented voice.

"True," the prince replied, "see the number of people who have turned up today to wish her well on her journey."

"Why do you think so many people wish to honour her?"

The prince was somewhat surprised by the question and could only respond by saying "because she was the Pharaoh, and because she was loved."

"Indeed, sir," responded the Scholar with a slight smile, although he knew this was not the main reason. In Egyptian society the number of mourners at a person's funeral reflected their status within the community, but even allowing for this - and that the status of Pharaoh could not be higher - numbers had far exceeded expectations.

"Please tell me how I should address you?" The prince was eager to make progress. "My mother said you are called the True Scholar or the Sage, but you must have a name."

"Oh I have sir, but I also had a father with, I think, a strange sense of humour. The name he gave me was in honour of several dynasties of your ancestors. It is Hatshepsutsobeknofrumeryt-neith."

"All women?" queried the prince, raising an eyebrow.

"All women!" confirmed the scholar. "Fortunately, as I have grown in years, I have been honoured with the title Sage…"

"Or True Scholar" interrupted the prince.

"…or True Scholar, although your mother always addressed me by my family name, Prem, which was my preference as I am not an enthusiastic adopter of titles."

"Then," said the prince "I think we'll use that."

He continued. "My mother told me before she died, that I should come and talk to you. I believe that you sometimes offered her advice."

"I had that honour sir. Your grandfather's orders ensured that I could not visit the court until after his death but my wife was, for a time, handmaiden to your mother and, I think, also a friend. Through her, I was privileged to be introduced to your mother and, on occasion, offer her counsel."

"Will you give the same service to me?" asked the prince.

"When you are ready sir, for you have a great deal to do in the next few months. I will be happy to speak to you when the time is right," again he bowed to the younger man.

"Then I will contact you," said Smendes.

Prem knew this was untrue. He also knew that if the prince was aware of just one of the secrets of the pyramid journey, he would understand the reason for the huge attendance at his mother's funeral. However, now was not the time to challenge the young man's thinking and explain the secret. Instead, he handed Smendes a small scroll containing his personal details and the inscription:

'True scholars are those who give what they have without meanness and without secret.'

Smendes was bemused, but shook the Sage's hand whilst thinking to himself that the words might indicate some arrogance on the part of his new acquaintance.

BEGINNINGS

The coronation took place and Smendes was crowned Pharaoh, supreme ruler of his people and the most important and powerful man in all of Egypt.

He began his reign in the manner in which all previous Pharaohs had begun theirs, holding meetings and conferences with his high officials in order to become familiar with the status of his kingdom.

The first twelve months were devoted to supporting what was already in place and, although this helped the Pharaoh confront his new role, he was eager to start making his own mark on his kingdom.

He remembered his mother's advice to look after the people, build the pyramid right away and consult with the Sage.

Regarding the people he felt that, as long as he continued with his mother's policies, this would be sufficient. He had no need to change anything. He recalled the large numbers at the funeral and his officials assured him that the people were happy and content.

He would concentrate his efforts on the building of his pyramid and would begin that journey later on in the year. Contrary to his mother's advice, he did not intend to involve Prem – after all, why should he?

As prince, he had been trained for the role of Pharaoh and had spent many hours in the company of his mother and her advisers, listening to them as they planned her pyramid.

He knew more about pyramid building than any scholar did.

His instincts told him that he had to focus on just three things. First choose the correct site, second build the Pyramid and third decide the contents to be placed alongside him for the journey to the New World. Building the Pyramid was, to him, as simple as that.

The new Pharaoh had learnt much from his mother, regularly visiting her pyramid site, attending progress meetings and listening to the hundreds of officials, experts and specialists involved in the construction. He had experienced the building of the Pyramid for himself and, as he recalled, he had never seen the Sage at any stage of the construction. There was therefore no need to consult him in the building of his own pyramid.

He spent the remainder of the year assembling his team of managers and advisers, arguably the most important part of his planning process. He had learnt that the strength of this team would reflect the strength of his workforce and, ultimately, the quality and standard of his pyramid.

As he did so, he often remembered more of his mother's words: 'When the governing class isn't chosen for quality, it is chosen for material wealth. This always means decadence, the lowest stage a society can reach'.

His team would include a mixture of youth and experience. Some of his mother's people would be invited to take up positions on the project, but the new Pharaoh felt that, in order for him to complete the Pyramid, new blood would be required.

He started with the appointment of his architect, an expert in pyramid design and a man so devoted to his vocation that he had earned the reputation as the expert in his field. The Pharaoh asked him to challenge previous creations and design a monument so impressive that it would inspire and amaze the world.

In response to this the architect had launched into a lengthy discourse about the grandeur of the structure he envisaged and how he would create a memorial that would last through the ages.

Eyes half closed in an ecstasy of creative thought, the Pharaoh's appointed draughtsman talked on and on about the project and, more and more, about his own talents and abilities.

At one point, Smendes actually left the room for some moments and, on his return, found the architect still talking, apparently unaware that his king had not been present.

"Creative types," muttered the Pharaoh to himself, after a lengthy and rather one-sided meeting. "It's a wonder they come down to earth for long enough to build anything."

Other appointments followed swiftly and, to the Pharaoh's relief, with rather less fuss.

A team of specialists and scholars covering disciplines such as tool making, food, clothing, safety, storage and security supported his senior advisers. Scribes were also appointed to document the progress made on the journey and to produce regular reports for the Pharaoh.

In keeping with his mother's advice to look after the people, he appointed an expert to attend to the needs of the workforce.

During the time that these appointments were being made, one of the older advisers asked the Pharaoh if a plan would be produced to help focus everyones' minds on their great task.

The Pharaoh replied that he had confidence in their abilities, that there was no need to spend time on an unnecessary exercise and, more importantly, that it was not in a Pharaoh's nature to produce a plan. A Pharaoh had, to the best of his knowledge, never produced a plan before and he wasn't about to start now.

He also quoted from a discussion he had with one of the scholars from his mother's reign when he was told 'all we need is the same knowledge, the same experience and we will achieve the same result'. That was good enough for Smendes.

The following morning he announced to the people of Egypt that they were about to embark on a new journey, to build the Pharaoh's Pyramid.

CONSTRUCTION COMMENCES

The building of the Pyramid got off to a great start. The people were delighted that they were embarking on the new Pharaoh's journey and were keen to demonstrate their support for their king.

The architect had, true to his word, designed the perfect pyramid and, with the help of astronomers, had found the ideal location, a factor key in property choice even then.

The building of the Pyramid was to involve six phases and the architect knew that the first, laying the foundations, was the most important. This would take at least two years to complete and the people set about the task with energy and enthusiasm.

Egyptians had a high respect for order and there was no doubt that the construction operation was organised and well managed.

Fifteen hundred men were placed at the quarry site. Skilled stonemasons, master craftsmen working with copper chisels, produced blocks of stone from the mountainside. The chatter from the masons and the sound of the chisels on stone, and on the occasional thumb, was both consistent and deafening. All were impressed by the commitment to the Pharaoh's cause.

Finished blocks were placed on wooden sledges, requiring up to two hundred people to manoeuvre them, and pulled on land or shipped up the Nile to the pyramid site.

At the pyramid site, the excavation work matched the pace at the quarry as the land was cleared, then levelled in preparation for the delivery of the stone.

Two years later, and according to the schedule agreed with the Pharaoh, the first phase was completed. The foundations were laid and now the hard work was about to begin. This would involve more stone, more transport and considerably more people – an extra seventeen thousand in total.

The Pharaoh called for the people of Egypt to support the next stage of the pyramid construction. Conscription had existed within the kingdom for many years and it was every Egyptian's duty to enlist. This meant that it wasn't going to be difficult to enrol the labour required in order to complete the Pyramid.

At least that was the theory.

The Pharaoh anticipated a positive response but, to his horror and surprise, found that only two thousand people supported his call to action. This would take the total workforce to five thousand, far short of the figure needed to complete the work on time.

The royal advisers were as surprised as the Pharaoh at the low response but, as they were too involved in their day-to-day jobs, were unable to understand or explain the reasons why. To say that the Pharaoh was unimpressed was an understatement.

Three intense weeks were spent in further recruitment and reminding reluctant citizens of their obligations. At the end of that period the workforce was up to strength, although there was still no real explanation for the initial reluctance to join up.

The Pharaoh could now relax, confident that pyramid construction would remain on schedule. It was two and a half years since they started the journey but it seemed to him just days ago.

The work picked up pace. Everyone played his or her part and the Pyramid began to take shape. From its level base, the completed monument would include two hundred courses of stone, each one smaller than the last. In the next year, three courses would be completed.

One day the Pharaoh decided to visit the quarry and then the pyramid site to check the progress. He had chaired many meetings with his managers and advisers over the year and reports on the construction had been encouraging. The journey was ahead of schedule and the people were happy. It was time for the Pharaoh to see for himself.

He was delighted with the progress made and he decided to extend the visit and greet the people personally. Everyone seemed happy and, when asked, told the Pharaoh that all was well.

He returned to the palace a contented man and the advisers attending him breathed a sigh of relief, for an unhappy Pharaoh was not considered conducive to a long and happy life.

The harsh truth was that, although the people may have had the appearance of being busy, they were, like the workers who disposed of the sewage from the teams of animals used on the project, merely going through the motions.

They were supporting the Pharaoh's journey with a reasonable standard of work but the passion and pride was missing. They knew in their hearts that they had to support the journey, but they had serious reservations about the new Pharaoh.

Many found him abrupt, cold and aloof. He didn't seem to have the humanity that his mother had. They also felt isolated from him. Since the coronation he had left his palace only twice to meet them. As a result, rumours began to surface regarding his intentions for the kingdom. People were unsure of his plans for the future. War with Egypt's neighbours was constantly talked about and people feared a return to the bad old days when his grandfather had ruled.

At a personal level, the people also saw, and were affected by, some small but significant changes. Food wasn't quite as plentiful as it had been and, although there wasn't a major crisis, it was commonplace to go several weeks without certain foodstuffs. This surprised the people, as they believed Egypt to be the wealthiest country in the world.

Wives spent less time with their husbands, children saw less of their fathers. Families were being affected by the long hours the men spent on the construction of the Pyramid. Rest days were rare and many people worked from dawn until dusk. It was not surprising to find family relationships strained, and the new Pharaoh was to blame.

It had never been like this under the reign of his mother.

Many people also felt fear. They remembered his wild days as a younger man and stories circulated that he would punish those who had then criticised him. They expected him now, as Pharaoh, to be true to his word.

They vented their frustrations on their superiors who, in turn, notified the Pharaoh's advisers. Nobody, however, was brave or confident enough to inform the Pharaoh of the people's concerns. Instead, they tried to manage the workforce individually or collectively, with a mixed degree of success.

Their approach was to remind the workers of their duty to the King but this only caused further dissent. They were well aware of their duty but, quite simply, their hearts were not in the pyramid journey.

Ironically, the Pharaoh's last visit to the site had increased the work rate for a few days but then it slid back at an alarming rate. Eventually, the building of the Pyramid fell behind schedule.

It was now four years into the journey and the new Pharaoh was no longer new. Smendes summoned an urgent meeting of his managers and advisers. He reminded them in no uncertain terms that, as ruler of Egypt, he was able to command his people to move mountains.

"So why are you unable to get your people to carve, move and place a few pieces of stone?" he asked them.

This was a deeply insulting remark. It understated the complexity and size of the project and, at the same time, undervalued the advisers and other officials as individuals.

He asked them each to list the various problems linked to their areas of responsibility and, when they did so, he responded by offering them solutions to bring the construction back on schedule. The mood of the meeting was both tense and quiet. The team were frightened to speak out and offer any input to the process. This only made the Pharaoh angrier.

"Tell the people they have a duty to their Pharaoh!" he shouted. Then, for the first time, the team witnessed for themselves behaviour from the Pharaoh they never thought they would see. He personally ridiculed them, questioned their ability and blamed them for the situation he was in. Even the architect wasn't excused from the criticism, and those closest to him saw a tear well in his sensitive eye.

One of the scribes was told to complete a detailed summary of the Pharaoh's required actions, including who was responsible and the timescales involved. The meeting concluded when he informed them that failure would not be tolerated. He also told them to communicate his concerns to their workers.

The officials left the meeting angry, frustrated and bewildered from the experience. Many feared for their jobs, and some for their lives. By the end of the day, twenty thousand people were aware of the Pharaoh's mood.

Nevertheless, this made no difference to the construction schedule. The people arrived each day for work but their performance deteriorated and the pyramid construction fell further behind schedule.

The Pharaoh responded in the only way he knew. He consulted his advisers again but they could offer nothing new and half the team were dismissed. Bringing in new blood would, he believed, make a difference. However, the harder the team of managers and advisers worked, and the more time they spent with each other to try and resolve the situation, the more frustrated and ineffective they became. The pyramid building journey had reached a near standstill.

Matters came to a head when the Pharaoh contracted a serious illness.

The Royal Physician felt it was due to the stress Smendes was under and, although he assured the Pharaoh he would make a full recovery in time, the Pharaoh was convinced he was going to die. If he did, he would be unable to enter the New World. He had no Pyramid. He would go down in history as the unachieving Pharaoh.

For days he drifted in and out of consciousness, constantly experiencing nightmares involving his rejection at the door of the god Osiris. She refused to let him enter her kingdom. He was a failure. On the door to the New World was the inscription:

'If one tries to navigate unknown waters, one runs the risk of shipwreck'.

When his fever eventually subsided he woke up and realised that enough was enough.

He would have to pay Prem a visit.

THE FIRST MEETING

When the Pharaoh announced to his officials that he was going to meet with Prem, there was a huge sigh of relief. Like the Pharaoh, they didn't fully understand what one individual could bring to the journey, but if he were able to take the pressure off them his contribution would be worthwhile.

In advance of the meeting, the Pharaoh spent some time investigating the Sage's background. He found out he was the same age as his mother had been when she died, had a wife called NetBirdy and a daughter, Tor.

He had spent much time abroad but in the past thirty-five years had been based predominantly in Egypt. He was born in another land, as was his wife, and it was possibly for this reason that the other scholars in the kingdom did not warm to him.

Prem's education was very different from the Egyptian tradition and was based on knowledge, skill and experience amassed over many years. Trial and error played a key part in his early work. Learning from mistakes shaped his thinking. Learning from books did not.

He apparently prided himself on being a practitioner rather than a theorist and his methods had stood him in good stead for many years. This had earned him the titles of Sage and True Scholar, bestowed by the Pharaoh's mother

These were titles that many of the other scholars in Egypt didn't like, even though Prem himself did not appear to actually use them.

Neither did they understand what his contribution to the kingdom had been. They preferred to call him 'the foreign scholar', or the 'man of few words'. Very few respected his experience and supposed talent, although he did seem to enjoy a good relationship with a select group of scribes and students in and around the Pharaoh's Palace.

Prem himself referred to this group as 'the future of Egypt'. He believed that they held the perfect blend of Egyptian education, personal talent and his own pragmatic style.

They would often come to his house to learn about Egypt's past and to discuss the future. They always left inspired. They also believed that they had the best personal coach and mentor in all of Egypt. However, this exclusive band of men and women were in the minority.

Rather than summon Prem to the Royal Palace, the Pharaoh thought a visit to him at his home would enable him to gain a better understanding of the man.

Arrangements were made and, when the Pharaoh arrived at Prem's house, he was struck by its modesty and simplicity.

Smendes was ushered into the house by a tiny wrinkled woman who seemed rather overwhelmed by the royal presence.

She bowed as low as her ancient back would permit and fixed her gaze on the floor as she walked ahead of Smendes, this resulting in her ricocheting off several items of furniture during their progress.

On reaching the main reception room of the house the old woman retreated, still bowing and now walking backwards. After several attempts, she succeeded in backing through the door.

Oddly, there was no sign of Prem or any member of his family, although the Pharaoh was obviously expected. Now the King might have taken offence at this slight but, instead, he was more intrigued by the contents of the room.

Like the hall he had just passed through, the floor was covered in an apparently random selection of rugs. Perhaps these had been what the elderly servant had been studying. Such was the profusion of rugs in the reception room that the ceiling seemed several fingerbreadths lower than it had in the hall.

Against the walls were seemingly countless shelves containing heaps of papyrus scrolls.

Surveying these as he inspected the room the Pharaoh passed a window, through which he could see Prem and two women, presumably his wife and daughter, in the garden.

What they were doing was a mystery. The tall figure occasionally pointed a long, thin finger at a bed of flowers or shrubs, which the two women would then rush into, frequently making small leaps into the air accompanied by squeals of mock alarm and laughter.

Turning his attention back to the room, Smendes picked up several scrolls at random. Many were in languages foreign to him, but all those written in the hieroglyphs that he could read seemed to be votes of thanks and letters of gratitude to the Sage.

Other than the rugs and the scrolls, it was obvious that someone within the home was fond of hippopotami. Carvings, models and illustrations of the animals covered almost every free surface. Smendes examined several of these in the continuing absence of his host.

As with the scrolls, these all seemed to be tokens of thanks, each bearing some sort of text or dedication. Turning one of them idly in his hands, the Pharaoh again looked out of the window opening. The garden was now empty although, curiously, a length of red ribbon was making its way through the grass, seemingly of its own volition.

Before he could give further thought to this phenomenon, he became aware of another presence in the room and, turning, saw Prem bowing from the doorway. Behind him were the two women from the garden.

"You honour us with your visit, sir."

The Pharaoh nodded his head in acknowledgement, his eyes taking in the two figures standing behind the Sage.

"May I introduce my wife and daughter?"

The Pharaoh smiled: "NetBirdy and Tor. I have heard your names and I am honoured."

For this, he was rewarded by a broad smile from Prem's wife, whilst the daughter blushed and seemed, of a sudden, to find her feet of great interest.

Perhaps she's been coached by the old servant woman, thought Smendes.

Prem gestured at the hippopotamus carving in the Pharaoh's hand. "I'm afraid we have an infestation of the creatures, sir. I seem to acquire them on a regular basis although, fortunately, my wife and daughter are fond of the beasts."

This remark was rewarded by an even broader grin from NetBirdy, whilst Tor blushed more deeply than before.

The Pharaoh could see that Prem was devoted to his wife, a small, slim woman who seemed constantly amused, as if she knew something that the rest of the world did not.

"Do either of you practice sorcery?" asked the Pharaoh. "Earlier, I saw a ribbon of cloth moving across your garden, seemingly by itself, for there is no breeze."

Tor and NetBirdy exchanged looks of alarm and rushed from the room.

Prem smiled. "My wife has had a pet for many years, one that belonged to a friend of hers before that. It is a humble tortoise, sir, but one that has proved to be no respecter of even royal feet in the past.

"It is the custom of her people to gently restrain such errant creatures with ribbon, evidently, in this case, with little success."

During the rest of the Pharaoh's visit, he could hear the two women in other rooms or in the cool, shady garden. They would constantly chatter and laugh at each other's jokes and, indeed, they appeared to be more like sisters than mother and daughter. Overall, the house was a picture of love, happiness and tranquillity.

After the initial greetings and refreshments, Prem invited the Pharaoh into his office at the back of the house. The walls were again covered, this time with messages from previous Pharaohs, other leaders and, it appeared, followers of Prem.

Two in particular set the tone for these. They read:

'Love is one thing, knowledge is another'

and

'If you would build something solid, don't work with the wind; always look for a fixed point, something you know that is stable...yourself'.

They also featured framed inscriptions with a consistent theme throughout making mention of 'the journey'. There was one large frame in particular, which made reference to 'the formula'. Even after he had looked at much that was on display, the Pharaoh still couldn't work out what Prem's vocation actually was.

The Sage attempted to explain some of the meanings behind the inscriptions but the Pharaoh was more interested in getting to the point of the meeting.

"What do you actually do?" he asked, pointing to the displays on each wall. "These are all fascinating but what do they mean?"

Prem thought for a few moments.

"All of my clients are on a journey of some sort: a journey of discovery, a journey of creation, a journey of personal growth. My job is to help and guide them throughout that journey and to ensure that they reach their chosen destination on time."

The Pharaoh was none the wiser and asked him to elaborate.

Prem continued. "The people I work with have an idea, a dream or an ambition that they would like to realise. They surround themselves with other people who they trust will support them in their endeavour. They are ambitious, positive and energetic men and women. Unfortunately, on their journey, they encounter difficulties, challenges and frustrations that could prevent them from reaching their ultimate destination. My role is to help them minimise the difficulties, avoid many of the frustrations and overcome the challenges on the journey.

"In your case you are striving to construct the perfect pyramid. I also know that you are behind schedule and you face many challenges at the moment. You will face many more in the future."

The Pharaoh placed his hands on the Sage's shoulders in an almost fraternal gesture. "Will you build the Pyramid for me?"

"That I cannot do, sir, but what I will do is work with you to make sure that it happens."

"What good is that to me?" demanded the Pharaoh. "I have nearly twenty thousand people already working with me to build the Pyramid. Another person will make no difference."

"I beg to differ," was the reply. "First of all the people are not working with you, they merely give the appearance of doing so; they are unsure of your motives. There are rumours of future war and, forgive me saying so, but many of the people don't like you." He continued. "They are working on the pyramid construction not because they want to, but out of a sense of duty. Secondly, I can make a difference to the construction but only if you believe that I can. You have already asked your people to take a leap of faith in you; well I'm asking you to do the same. Have faith in my ability to help you realise your dream."

Prem's frankness staggered the Pharaoh. He was not used to such forthright opinions and, worse, felt wounded by these insights. He could only respond with anger.

"Then you too can work on the Pyramid out of a sense of duty! I don't know why I came here to ask for your help. I am commanding you to help me. I am the Pharaoh, the supreme ruler of Egypt and I expect you to do as I say. There will be no leap of faith. I expect you to help."

The Sage gestured to a nearby couch and, when the Pharaoh refused his invitation, he sat down instead. "Forgive my directness, but I imagine that the way you have just spoken to me is the same manner in which you have spoken to your managers and advisers. It is little wonder that morale in the kingdom is so low."

The Pharaoh showed surprise, but this didn't deter Prem. He continued, "In truth, I am not an Egyptian subject, neither are my wife or daughter. I am not obliged to help you in the building of your pyramid, although I would like to do so."

The Pharaoh was not used to such obstinate behaviour. "You may not be Egyptian but you must have had a sense of duty to our kingdom in the past or you would never have helped my mother."

"Again you are incorrect sir. I helped your mother because I wanted to, not because I was forced. There is a marked difference."

The discussion was going nowhere, although the Pharaoh had to admit that Prem had a point. Perhaps, he thought, the people of Egypt were really working on the Pyramid because they had to and not because they wanted to. Perhaps this was the main reason why the construction was behind schedule.

"Your mother and I had a fine relationship thanks, in no small part, to my wife's friendship with her. We both worked hard and we enjoyed each other's company. We achieved a lot and, in our time together, she never once commanded me to help her. It was an honour and a privilege to work with her."

"Very well" said the Pharaoh, his temper cooling slightly, "when you said 'have faith in you', what did you mean?"

"I know the six stages to building the Pyramid."

The Pharaoh interrupted him. "You know the six stages! I thought they were supposed to be secret. Only the Pharaoh, the architect and a few trusted followers know about them."

"I'm not talking about the six phases to the construction of the Pyramid. I am referring to the formula; the six stages designed to ensure that the pyramid building journey is completed satisfactorily and on time. They are very different."

The Pharaoh was confused. He knew that the construction of the Pyramid had secrets. Now he had found out that Prem had additional secrets that, it seemed, help on the journey. Why had his mother not told him? But perhaps she had, after all. Hadn't she said 'The True Scholar has the formula'.

"But why your secrets?" asked the Pharaoh "What is so special about these six stages that nobody knows them but you?"

Prem rose from his couch.

"I will explain all of this in due time, but for now I must ask you to trust me. I share the same desire as you to complete your journey successfully. How do you think I have earned my reputation over the years? Only by sharing my secrets with others. Trust me, and I will share all of them with you."

The Pharaoh relaxed somewhat and Prem continued.

"I believe that, for the journey to be completed successfully, we have to understand and respect each other's roles. You know more about pyramid building than I could ever dream of and, since you were a child, you have been groomed to be Pharaoh.

"You have been trained on matters of state and matters of war. You were born to be King. Part of your training meant understanding how a pyramid should be constructed. You also know that, over the generations, each newly crowned Pharaoh has tried to improve on the design and construction of his or her pyramid. The pyramid built for your mother was many times finer than those that went before.

"I have no right to tell you how your pyramid should be built. That is your responsibility. I also don't have a right to comment on the quality of your advisers. They are your appointments and in time you will find out, as previous Pharaoh's have, whether they are right for the journey.

"I do know one thing though, and that is that you have made the best possible decisions on your journey based on the information you have to hand. You should be pleased with what you have achieved to date, but your journey is only beginning."

The Pharaoh was beginning to warm to this strange and outspoken man.

"Although I don't have a right to advise you on how to build your pyramid, I do have a duty to assist you on your journey, but only if you agree to my philosophies, methods and approaches."

"What do you mean?" asked the Pharaoh.

"The leap of faith involves the use of the formula, the six stages to success on your pyramid building journey. That's the easy part, but have a look at this." He guided the Pharaoh over to a framed inscription on the wall. It read:

'You don't know what you don't know!'

"Consider the inscription for a moment. Any Pharaoh is only as good as the knowledge, experience and skill gained over their years as ruler of their kingdom. You yourself had a great upbringing. You were trained from an early age to be Pharaoh. You were surrounded by accomplished scribes and scholars who taught you just about everything you know. Your mother also taught you a great deal. But you still don't know what you don't know.

"Tomorrow you will learn more, and the next day and the next. Adopting the philosophy 'you don't know what you don't know' will be critical to the relationship we have together and the success we enjoy on the pyramid building journey."

The Pharaoh thought for a few moments and, whilst in agreement with the sentiments within the inscription, said "but surely this also applies to you. You don't know what you don't know!"

"Exactly," Prem began to pace the room as he continued. "It applies equally to me. The six stages that make up the formula have been developed over many years, working with many people. The secrets within each stage include the best possible advice I am able to offer you today. I can guarantee though, that the knowledge I will have gained in five years' time, based on my experiences with you on your journey, will also help me be a more proficient scholar.

"Consequently, my advice to others in the future will be even better, but that is the great thing about my work. I help people build pyramids and I learn something new each day. I am then able to keep adding something more valuable to the formula. I am able to pass the secrets on to others. Everyone then benefits. I am not all-knowing, but merely act as a channel for much accumulated wisdom."

The Pharaoh smiled and suggested that they forget their bad start and that it might be a good idea to begin again. Prem agreed.

Together they wandered into the garden where, in the lush grass, something dark, domed and unfettered stirred.

"How often would we meet and work together? Will you tell me the six stages today? How will I know that they are working?" the Pharaoh had so many questions to ask and was impatient to get started on the journey. Prem replied that the six stages would be revealed over the lifespan of the journey and that the outcomes of each stage would be clearly visible. He wouldn't need to look far to see if they were working or not, but this would be covered at a later date.

"We can meet as often or as little as you wish after we have successfully completed the first two stages of the formula. You will decide the frequency and the length of the meetings and sessions. All I ask is that you are prepared to answer and discuss the following questions at each session we have together:

What has happened on the journey since our previous meeting?

What have you personally learnt from the experience?

What are the new challenges that you now face?

What would you like to know to help you on the next leg of the journey?"

The Pharaoh considered these requirements. They seemed straightforward, and he was secretly pleased that their meetings would have a structure to them.

"I have so much information I could share with you regarding your journey that it will be easier for both of us if you come fully prepared. Ask me as many questions as you wish and I will do my best to give you an answer by way of knowledge, skill, support and help."

"Remember, sir, it is as much in my interest as it is yours to complete the journey successfully."

"Very well, but here's a question for you" replied the Pharaoh. "Why don't you just tell me the six stages now? It would save a great deal of time, and would enable me to bring the journey back on schedule."

Prem smiled and pointed again to the inscription 'You don't know what you don't know'.

"I see" said the Pharaoh, somewhat resignedly, "and I imagine there must be a valid reason that will become apparent in due course."

The Pharaoh was happy to concede the point, but he wasn't quite finished. He needed some reassurance that Prem was capable of this undertaking. The building of the Pyramid was probably the biggest single task the Pharaoh would undertake in his reign and, if he was about to place his faith in a comparative stranger, he needed some evidence that the man knew what he was taking on. Prem was yet to pass the Pharaoh's personal test and so, not unreasonably, the king asked for some evidence of his record of achievement.

The request made Prem quite defensive.

"I don't mean to be disrespectful your Royal Highness, but I don't believe that I need to prove my worth. I have built many pyramids for many people over the years and you are the fourth ruler of Egypt I have lived under. I have also worked on three specific Pharaoh Pyramids as a young man and in my middle age. Two Pharaohs took my advice and were successful on their journey. One, your Grandfather, did not and his reign ended in disaster. You have to decide if I am right for you and your team. I would be delighted to work with you, but the decision is yours."

The Pharaoh heard the words but he wouldn't be swayed. He needed practical evidence.

Prem continued. "Please remember, sir, that you came to me. You have many issues that have to be addressed and I know I can help you. You have the potential to be a greater Pharaoh than even your mother was and I would like to be part of your journey, but I believe that I do not need to justifying myself to you. I believe my record speaks for itself."

"Your flattery is noted," replied the Pharaoh, "but surely you must concede that I will be announcing your input to my advisers, and they will need to be convinced that you understand the issues that we currently face. Very few of them know you and none that I know of have discussed working with you."

The Pharaoh had made a valid point. Prem also recognised that, for the journey to be successful, he would need the support of the Pharaoh's team of advisers and managers. Alienating them at the beginning of the journey would not be a good start. He had to give the Pharaoh something to take back to his team. He opened a chest and gave Smendes a sealed document. "Will this help?" he asked.

The Pharaoh opened the document. It was entitled 'The Challenges Faced on the Pyramid Building Journey'. It listed a number of factors, which had to be addressed by the Pharaoh and the people of Egypt if the journey was to be completed successfully.

Prem took the document back for a few moments and, again, addressed the Pharaoh. As he spoke, he occasionally glanced at the document.

"Over the years, I have learnt that building a pyramid involves a number of challenges, all of which test the dedication of everyone involved.

"To fund construction, trade will have to be maintained and, throughout the years of the construction journey, improvements in efficiency will have to be made. The people working on the project will also need constant training to develop skills, perhaps helped by people not themselves involved in the work.

"There will be high and low points on the journey and, to compensate for these, communication with the workforce is vital."

He looked directly into the Pharaoh's eyes.

"Two of your biggest challenges, sir, will be to gain the support of your people to the project, and to manage the change needed to complete the journey, a journey that will affect everyone, from the highest to the lowest in the land."

He passed the document back to the Pharaoh.

"Understand these challenges, produce a plan accordingly and success will be yours."

The Pharaoh was impressed. He clasped Prem's hand and thanked him for his time. He now had something to go back to his advisers and counsellors with. He also had to decide whether to place his faith in the man his mother had been pleased to call the Sage.

On the way back to the palace the Pharaoh was in a reflective mood. He now had a better understanding of Prem, his potential role and his levels of expertise. He was an expert in the completion of journeys. He had given the Pharaoh a promise that he would guide and support him throughout his own personal journey. He looked forward to that input. The inscription also impressed him

'You don't know what you don't know.'

He wondered why none of his other scholars had ever made mention of this.

Prem had indicated that he would challenge the Pharaoh's thinking, his ideas, values and the purpose of the journey. He wasn't going to admit it to anyone, but he didn't like the sound of that. He was, off course, the Pharaoh, the supreme ruler of Egypt and the most important man in the kingdom. He wasn't used to being challenged.

He also knew that there were hundreds of scholars to choose from within the kingdom but there was no one experienced or specialised in the completion of journeys.

When he arrived back at the palace, he made his decision. Whilst a physician attended to a small but painful bite on the Pharaoh's left foot, orders were given to despatch a servant to the Sage's house with this message. 'I will see you in two days to begin the journey. I look forward to learning about the formula'.

LAYING NEW FOUNDATIONS

The Pharaoh announced to his senior team of advisers that Prem would be helping them to build the perfect pyramid. He went on to explain that the man was a specialist in the completion of journeys. This was rewarded by a quizzical look from the majority of people at the meeting. They had never heard of the term in this context. Several of the scholars just smiled. They believed it was a term designed to create a mystique around Prem. In time, they would find out if this were true.

"Be assured that he will not interfere in the day-to-day construction of the Pyramid," said Smendes "or, for that matter, have anything to do with the jobs of the senior team of advisers." This helped, many believing that the last thing they needed was a stranger offering opinions on how they should carry out their work.

Two brave members of the team asked the Pharaoh to clarify what Prem would bring to the pyramid building journey. The Pharaoh was reluctant to mention the six stages included in the formula, for fear of being asked more questions that he was unable to answer. He also didn't want to announce that, as Pharaoh, he was about to place great reliance on one man.

He asked the assembled company to trust him; all would be revealed in time and they would be involved in every aspect of the journey. There would, he told them, be no surprises.

"But how do we know if he understands the problems we face as a team?" asked the Trade Ambassador, nervously rolling and unrolling the copy of 'What Chariot?' he constantly carried with him. "I've never met the man, but from what I've heard he has an unconventional approach. He has had a different upbringing to Egyptian scholars, some of whom are part of our team in this room." The scholars nodded in agreement. "He's not even Egyptian," continued the Ambassador, "how could he possibly understand the importance of the Pyramid to us?"

The Trade Ambassador was clearly representing the majority view. They waited for the Pharaoh's response. He thought for a few moments.

"Consider this. If we always do what we always did, we will always get what we always got!" The team listened to the words and tried to make some sense of them.

Smendes continued. "We are two years behind schedule and you are unable to demonstrate to me how we can avoid disaster. The construction of the Pyramid is a most important project to the people of Egypt. It affects their lives on a daily basis. We have the potential to alienate everyone in the kingdom if we don't complete the journey successfully. An unfinished pyramid means no passage to the New World for the Pharaoh and this, in turn, means no passage to the Gods for each Egyptian when it is their time to pass on."

The team knew the Pharaoh was right and they hated being reminded of their failure as a team. "The reality is," continued the Pharaoh, "if we always do what we always did, we will always get what we always got. In this instance, it means low productivity from our people resulting in an unfinished pyramid. I can't allow this to happen and that's why we will be involving the Sage in the project."

The team couldn't disagree with the Pharaoh's logic. They knew that something had to change, but they didn't know what. They didn't have the answers and, because of that, were unable to question the Pharaoh's decision. The Pharaoh, however, sensed that the team needed more evidence from him to convince them of the importance of Prem's involvement.

"I have spoken to this Prem at length. Although he was not born and raised in Egypt, he has a good deal to offer our nation, and I am convinced that his knowledge and skill will complement our own. Working with him will make a difference to the outcome of the journey."

The Pharaoh then found himself repeating to the team the inscription from the wall of the Sage's house: *'You don't know what you don't know'*.

"It is incredibly naïve of us to assume that we have all the answers. If we did, then we wouldn't find ourselves in this predicament," said the Pharaoh. "We don't know what we don't know and, more importantly, here is a man who knows what we don't know, or so I believe."

"He gave me this," said the Pharaoh. He produced the document that had been presented to him, highlighting the main challenges faced by the team on their pyramid building journey. The document was passed around the table. Every member of the team read it and each was astonished by its insight.

"Is that enough" asked the Pharaoh "to convince you that he has a grasp of the issues we are facing?" Everyone in the room, except the scholars, agreed that it was indeed enough. For the scholars, actions would speak louder than words. Prem was yet to pass their test.

"I expect everyone here today to support the Sage. Work with him begins next week," ordered the Pharaoh.

The meeting closed and the Pharaoh was happy that the appointment had been announced to the team. He was also pleased with the team's reaction to the 'Challenges' document. He was also realistic enough to know that it would take time to gain the full support of everyone.

At the agreed date, and a little before time, Prem arrived at the Royal Palace for his first formal session with the Pharaoh.

"You're early," said the Pharaoh.

"I learnt from your mother that punctuality is the politeness of queens and kings" was the simple reply.

In advance of the meeting, Prem had asked the Pharaoh to prepare a detailed report of the pyramid project to date. The presentation took up the first part of the morning and included the composition of the Pharaoh's team, the current position of the journey in relation to the planned schedule, and the problems and difficulties faced to date.

The remainder of the morning was spent meeting each member of the team. The Pharaoh left Prem to meet team members individually, giving him an opportunity to explain to them what he meant by the 'Completion of Journeys'. Additionally, it offered the team members a chance to ask questions. By the end of the morning session there were many converts to the new adviser's approach.

Even the Trade Ambassador's mind was now on higher things than the latest chariot's specification and performance.

When they met for their midday meal the Pharaoh asked Prem what he thought of his team. The Sage was surprised by the question.

"You will recall from our first meeting that I told you that I had no right to comment on or judge members of your team on their ability or performance. They are your appointments and you need to determine their contribution to the cause. The journey will help you in that regard."

He was right, thought the Pharaoh. He had no need to ask him, but he felt it would be useful to have some reassurance regarding the effectiveness of his team. He had reservations about one or two people's commitment to the journey and thought that Prem would give him some of his thoughts for consideration. The Pharaoh dismissed the question and moved on, asking about the formula and what would be involved.

"Stage one of the formula is about research" Prem replied. "It is the most important stage in the overall process and where most journeys go wrong, at the beginning."

He related the stage to the Pharaoh's own pyramid construction process, stressing the importance of laying the correct foundations. Stage one of the formula would involve the development of a solid base, one that would enable the five other stages to be carried out successfully in the future.

Prem explained in some detail that stage one consisted of three elements, each separate in its own right but also interconnected that, when completed, would give the Pharaoh the solid foundation he required.

The three components of stage one would be discussed initially between Prem and the Pharaoh, then the Pharaoh and his team of advisers and officials. Clearly warming to his subject, Prem went on to explain the three reasons why journeys fail at the beginning.

1. The reasons for embarking on the journey are not instantly clear to the people who are asked to join it.

2. The challenges likely to be encountered throughout the journey are very rarely identified in advance of the start and communicated to the people.

3. The journey is not communicated and presented in a way in which the people can imagine what it will look like and mean to them.

He explained that a combination of the three factors resulted in a variety of negative and confusing responses from the people.

Taking point one first, if the reasons for embarking on the journey aren't clear enough, people will join the journey for the wrong reasons, sometimes out of a sense of duty, because it is expected or, perhaps, because they have been forced to. The Pharaoh listened with interest to this and realised that the inscription 'You don't know what you don't know' was a powerful message.

Prem then developed the second point. He explained that when the challenges were not identified in advance of the journey start and communicated then to the people, they will often expect the journey to be almost perfect and uneventful. He told the Pharaoh that when problems and difficulties occurred on the journey three things would happen. Firstly, the people would not be prepared physically and mentally to overcome the challenges. Secondly they would mistrust the leaders for not informing them at the beginning of the journey. Finally, instead of concentrating on the forward momentum of the journey, the people would become preoccupied with the next potential challenge.

He explained, "people don't like surprises. They prefer to know the good and the bad parts of the journey from the outset, that way they can prepare themselves."

The Pharaoh knew how true this was. He noticed that every time there was a problem, either at the quarry, in the desert or at the pyramid site, how easily the people became dismayed.

Prem went on to discuss the third point. He told the Pharaoh that, the stronger and more compelling his vision was, the easier it would be to enlist and sustain support and focus his people on the construction of the Pyramid. He also added that it would be a lot easier to counter the many difficulties he was likely to face in the coming years.

The Pharaoh tried to make sense of the three points and relate them to the mistakes he and his team had made at the beginning of the pyramid building journey. As he was thinking about them, Prem asked him to recollect how the journey was planned and then communicated to his people in the early days of his reign.

The Pharaoh recalled the events leading up to the announcement. He formed his team, had meetings with the architect, agreed in principle the idea of building the perfect pyramid and then asked his team to announce the plans to the Egyptian people. "It was as simple as that," said the Pharaoh.

"What message do you think the people heard from their leaders?" The Pharaoh struggled with the question. He knew what he had announced, but he had no idea of what the people heard.

Before he could actually respond, Prem rose to his feet and, arms spread wide, gave his version of the proclamation. "The Pharaoh has announced that we are going on a new journey to build the perfect pyramid. It is your duty to support him as your new ruler. Enlist right away and ensure that he has the transport available to meet the Sun God Osiris when his time comes to leave the Old World."

"And what's wrong with that?" asked the Pharaoh.

"Well let's consider those words" replied Prem, "we are going...it is your duty...enlist now...ensure..." The Pharaoh knew what he was about to say.

"How do you think your people felt when they heard your proclamation, particularly when they were yet to meet you, see you, understand you and be given an opportunity to support you?"

The Pharaoh understood the point he was making. It was too direct, too dominating, and too aggressive. It also lacked the personal touch; it was selfish and focused totally on his needs. It disregarded the needs and aspirations of his people. It was an instruction, a command, rather than a vision that they could be part of. Smendes felt despondent.

Prem noticed his reaction and tried to raise his spirits. He explained that the Pharaoh's announcement to his people was well meant, but that he had not involved the people in the planning stage. This was a common mistake made by Pharaohs in the past who were in too much of a hurry to complete the journey.

Planning the communication at the beginning of the journey had been neglected. The Pharaoh replied that he never at any time meant to alienate his people, quite the reverse. He had wanted to have his people's support in what he believed was a worthy cause. In his haste, his words had rebounded on him. He also realised why he received such a poor response to his call to action.

Prem cheerfully assured him that all was not lost, and that they would soon make up lost ground.

To obtain support from his people on the journey he would have to carry out additional work with his team, based on the three points discussed earlier. The Pharaoh was asked to:

1. Agree what Prem called the imperatives for growth, the six main reasons why the people of Egypt should embark on the Pharaoh's journey. This information would be used to earn commitment from his people to the journey. It would also be used to enlist new people in the future.

2. Identify the anticipated challenges and hurdles that the Pharaoh and his team were likely to encounter throughout the journey.

3. Produce a vision of what the journey would look like for everyone in Egypt. In conjunction with the imperatives for growth, the vision would be used to inspire people to support the journey, play a personal part in the realisation of the Pharaoh's dream and overcome any challenges and obstacles.

Prem assured the Pharaoh that the outcomes produced from the work would form part of what he called the 'Journey Map', which would be used by the Pharaoh's team of advisers and managers to lead and guide the people over the time span of the pyramid construction. The Pharaoh liked the idea of the map but worried about the inclusion of the secrets relating to the construction of the Pyramid.

Further reassurance was offered to Smendes, in that the 'Journey Map' would never include the design and construction secrets of the Pyramid. It would instead focus on the outcomes from the use of the formula.

For the first time since they had met, the Pharaoh was truly energised by the guidance, advice and support he was receiving. He couldn't wait to get back to his team and complete the three pieces of work. He thanked Prem for his time, bade him farewell and set up a meeting with his team the following day. There was a lot to do.

Prem returned to the palace a few weeks later to review and discuss the team's work. The Pharaoh was unusually nervous. Not since he had spent time at school, had he been put in a position where his work was being reviewed. In truth, there was no need for anxiety. His team had worked long and hard and had produced three outstanding pieces of work. The Pharaoh handed the three documents to the Sage.

He opened and read the first document, the 'Imperatives for growth'. The team had highlighted six main reasons why they were embarking on the journey. The content included a sub-heading with a brief outline explaining each imperative.

THE PHARAOH'S JOURNEY INTO THE AFTERLIFE

The most important reason for us embarking on the journey. Our Pharaoh is a God. Only he can represent us and ensure that our dreams and ambitions can become a reality. Helping him on his journey into the Afterlife will benefit us all.

THE PASSAGE TO HEAVEN FOR ALL EGYPTIAN PEOPLE

Linked to the imperative highlighted above, our Pharaoh will talk to the Sun God Osiris on our behalf and will ensure that, when it is our time to pass onto the New World, our passage to heaven will have been prepared in advance for us.

EGYPT'S STATUS IN THE WORLD

As Egyptians, we pride ourselves in our status as the wealthiest country in the world. Everyone playing his or her personal part on the Pharaoh's Journey will ensure that our status will remain for generations to come.

THREATS

We know that our enemies are envious of our wealth and our success. Given an opportunity, they will attempt to steal our riches and rob us of our future. Building the Pharaoh's Pyramid will send a message to them that we are ready and willing to defend our nation.

FUTURE WEALTH AND SECURITY

Building the Pyramid and supporting the Pharaoh on his journey will ensure future wealth and security for our people. Our children and our children's children will benefit from the Pharaoh's journey.

APPROVAL FROM THE GODS

The Sun God Osiris has a high expectation of the people of Egypt, as do many other equally important Gods. We have a duty to worship them, support our Pharaoh and retain their approval of our wishes and dreams for our great kingdom.

Prem was impressed with the document, particularly the simplicity of the six statements. The use of the 'Imperatives for growth' was important to the success of the journey.

The second document was an amended version of the 'Challenges' document that had been presented to the Pharaoh. The team of advisers and managers had used it as the starting point for their own document. They had discussed and debated its merits in detail, amended where appropriate and produced a final version that reflected the Pharaoh's journey. In total, it included twelve challenges that they believed summarised the demands which would be placed on them.

- Sustaining and improving trade with other nations
- Improving productivity and efficiency throughout the pyramid construction
- Managing the Pharaoh's journey and the necessary change required
- Sustaining the Egyptian people's focus throughout the journey
- Recruiting new talent and expertise when the time was right
- Developing and promoting the benefits of the Pyramid
- Retaining existing talent within the Kingdom of Egypt
- Funding the resources required to succeed on the journey
- Developing new building systems and processes
- Communicating the journey's progress to everyone in the kingdom
- Improving the knowledge and skills of the Egyptian people
- Gaining widespread support to the Pharaoh's journey to the New World

Finally, Prem opened the 'Vision' document, the most important element of the 'Journey Map'. He read it several times.

Our overall vision is to create for our Pharaoh and the Kingdom of Egypt a monument that will transport our King to the heavens above where he will meet our Sun God Osiris in the New World. Our plan is to construct the perfect pyramid. This will be a structure unlike any built beforehand in terms of design, attention to detail and scale. It will be a truly impressive monument and a testament to the design and construction expertise of the people of Egypt. It will also be constructed to stand throughout the ages to come.

Future generations of people in Egypt and around the world will visit the Pharaoh's tomb and will marvel at the ingenuity and workmanship.

We aim to maintain the unique Egyptian cultural and construction traditions within the structure. The secrets of the Pyramid will continue to remain secret.

Every person in Egypt will play their part in its construction – at the quarry, on the pyramid site, in the deserts, the villages and by the banks of the Nile. Farmers supplying food to our people will be recognised and rewarded for their contribution to the journey as much as the craftsmen on the pyramid site or the high officials at our palaces around the kingdom.

The Pyramid will be known throughout the kingdom as a place to worship and a place at which to feel proud to be an Egyptian. On the journey to completion, our people will be supported in every way possible to ensure the Pyramid's successful and timely completion. Dedication, passion and teamwork will describe the core values of each person on the journey.

The culmination of the support by the people of Egypt will be the completion of the perfect pyramid ahead of the agreed schedule. The measurement of the nation's success will be the successful transportation of our Pharaoh from the Old World to the New World and the pride and satisfaction from each Egyptian, knowing that they played their part in his onward journey.

Prem put the three documents down on the table in front of him and congratulated the Pharaoh on a magnificent piece of work. The Pharaoh smiled and, for the first time on his pyramid building journey, felt a real sense of achievement. He knew there was a lot to do and that this was only the start, but what a start.

The Sage asked the Pharaoh what he had learnt from the past few weeks as he worked with his team on the three documents.

"That's easy" said the Pharaoh, "I've learnt that, contrary to what I believed before, we had never as a team discussed, developed or communicated properly the reasons why our people should join us on the journey. We just assumed that, because I was the new Pharaoh and that Pharaohs always build pyramids, they would understand the reasons and support the cause. We took the people for granted. We also forgot to communicate the broader reasons for the building of the Pyramid. We concentrated too much time on the journey to the New World and, whilst this is the main reason for the construction, there are five other equally important imperatives."

Prem thought that this was excellent.

The Pharaoh continued. "The 'Challenges' document was fairly straight forward. In the past, we would often discuss them on a personal level at great length, but we never agreed to take action as a group. We were so busy complaining about the issues and how they affected each other that we never thought to take stock, review them and then tackle them as a group.

"Working in isolation, we had no chance of overcoming them; as a group we now believe we can address them. Your list helped us focus on the entirety. We make no apologies for using your manuscript to produce our document."

Prem agreed.

"I've also learnt the importance of the vision. In truth, we have never had one before. What we had was my instruction to build. For the first time in my reign, we have something that we all believe is truly compelling. Our new vision touches the senses. When you read it you can almost hear, feel and see the journey. It appears more real. It reads and feels inspiring. As a team we are really proud of it. We can't wait to see the reaction of our people."

Prem once more concurred; it was a very impressive piece of work. "What have you learnt about your team and about yourself as a leader?"

"I am embarrassed to say," the Pharaoh replied, "that I now have a totally different view of my team of advisers and managers. I was first to blame them for the disarray, but the reality was that the blame lay totally with me. How could I have possibly expected them to complete this national project without any clear direction from myself? The problem didn't lie in their expertise or ability to carry out their job function. They are the right people for the job, they just lacked leadership from me. I'm also sorry to say that I've lost a few good people over the years, all because of my poor leadership. I was too quick to blame others."

"Don't be too hard on yourself," said Prem, smiling. "Your schooling taught you many things as a prince and, although your scholars coached you in the art of being a Pharaoh, it's a totally different experience when you hold the position and you are asked to lead your people. This is not the Old World, or the New World, this is the Real World."

"How true" replied the Pharaoh, "this is the real world and, although the training helped me, no one taught me the people side of the journey. No one taught me about your formula, including my mother."

"Don't be too hard on her either, everything she did was for a reason. Remember, you don't know what you don't know."

The Pharaoh laughed and Prem laughed with him.

"Where do we go from here?" asked the Pharaoh.

The Sage counselled the Pharaoh on his next course of action. He would be required to go back to his team, congratulate them on their outstanding work and to test the three documents with a few groups of people that Prem had in mind. The Pharaoh was asked if he would meet again in a month's time to discuss his findings.

THE MISSING DETAIL

When Prem arrived at the palace some weeks later the Pharaoh was, unusually, ready to greet him at the gates. This had never happened before. Normally a servant would come and collect the visitor from the palace entrance. The Pharaoh had never looked happier and was in a hurry to impart his good news. In line with the structure of the meetings they had agreed, he had produced a formal agenda and had planned in meticulous detail in readiness for Prem's arrival.

"I see, sir," said the Sage "that you are eager to tell me something."

The Pharaoh began by acquainting Prem with the latest news of the journey. Apparently word had been circulating of the Sage's involvement in the construction of the Pyramid and everyone in the Kingdom knew that he was working with the Pharaoh. Coincidentally, the construction had gained pace and had made significant progress, although it was still behind schedule. Reports from the supervisors around the sites indicated an increase in productivity, a reduction in sickness, an improvement in time keeping and, overall, a better spirit amongst the people.

The Pharaoh then moved on to tell Prem how pleased his team of advisers and officials were with the report he gave them from their last meeting regarding the completion of the 'Imperatives for growth', 'Challenges' and 'Vision' documents. Since then, he noticed how they had grown in stature, pride and self-confidence as a result of the successful completion of the work.

The presentation of the documents to the Egyptian people had also gone well. Prem had identified twenty teams across the four areas of the construction process to be part of a communication and discussion exercise, chaired by chosen officials.

The exercises were designed to gauge the initial reaction to the work from a sample of the Egyptian public and, at the same time, to learn lessons that could be used for the future. It seemed pointless, thought Prem, to launch the work to all of the Egyptian people without first testing it. Besides there was much more to do. The Pharaoh had agreed with his approach.

The Pharaoh began to outline to Prem the people's reaction to the three documents presented to them. He began with the imperatives for growth, the six reasons why they should embark on the Pharaoh's journey.

This document had the biggest impact on what the Pharaoh called the 'undecided'. They weren't negative people. They were people who were tired of having the importance of the Pharaoh's journey drummed into them. They had been told about it since they were children, the journey from the Old World to the New World. To them it wasn't news anymore and so, every time they heard a supervisor talk about their duty to support the Pharaoh's journey to the Afterlife, they didn't really listen.

One well-travelled official reporting back identified the state of mind of this group with a phrase that, he said, had its origins in a cloud-shrouded island far to the North of Egypt. It didn't translate very well, but included the words 'fed up' and 'back teeth'.

When, however, the people were presented with the full document, including the other five imperatives for growth, they began to realise its significance, particularly the reference to Egypt's status, its future wealth, security and the commitment to their children's future. Now that they had a better understanding of the reasons for the journey, they viewed the construction in a very different light.

Everyone else in the groups fully endorsed the imperatives for growth. Different imperatives appealed to different people and they could not wait to hear more from the Pharaoh's representatives at the meetings.

The Pharaoh then discussed the reaction to the 'Challenges' document. He explained that not everyone was initially interested in it, which he put down to the fact that they were focused purely on their day-to-day jobs. Many people could, however, see that the challenges related to every one of their job functions on the journey and were honest enough to say that they had never given much thought to the bigger picture within the country. Being presented with twelve future challenges linked to the overall kingdom seemed to interest only a few.

Prem acknowledged the point and made a mental note to revisit it in stage three of the journey. Everyone understanding that his or her contribution towards meeting the challenges was important to the success of the journey. He told the Pharaoh not to be concerned at the moment with the reactions. The fact that his team had identified them and were now presenting them to the people would reap benefits later on.

The Pharaoh did acknowledge that the people seemed to have renewed confidence in the leaders and advisers involved in the test sessions. He put this down to the open and honest way in which the documents were presented.

Smendes then moved onto the 'Vision' document. He explained that everyone received this part of the session remarkably well. There were no exceptions; the people were enthused and inspired by the presentation of the Pharaoh's vision. They were impressed for several reasons.

For the first time in his reign, the people had a clear idea of what the Pharaoh wanted to achieve in the kingdom. The new vision described, in a simple and straightforward manner, the Pharaoh's journey, what would be involved and what it would look like on completion. The people also liked the tone and the style of the 'Vision' document. They constantly referred to many of the words and phrases such as...the perfect pyramid...unlike any before...truly impressive...expertise of the people...will marvel and admire...feel proud to be an Egyptian...played their part in his onward journey.

They also commented that it looked like a vision that had been created by the people for the people. Everyone agreed that it was the most impressive piece of work they had ever seen. They also felt that, as Egyptians, they would be proud to serve their Pharaoh and ensure that the vision became a reality.

The Pharaoh put down his notes and beamed with delight.

"Wonderful news" said Prem, "and richly deserved. Your team put a lot of work into the documents." The Pharaoh agreed, and felt that the process to date had far exceeded his expectations.

"Let us then move on. What have you learnt personally from the experiences of the past few weeks?"

The Pharaoh explained that he had learnt a great deal from the planning and presentation experiences. He didn't wish to dwell on the mistakes of the past, particularly during the first two years of his reign, but he had learnt the importance of clarifying the reasons for embarking on the journey to his people. His learning also included identifying the challenges in advance of the journey and the importance of producing a truly compelling vision of the journey.

He realised that every person in Egypt - man, woman and child - has an experience of previous journeys. Perhaps it was on the Pharaoh's mother's journey, or that of his grandfather. Perhaps they had learnt about them from a brother, sister or parent but this journey was their first. No matter their age or experience, they would be carrying some good and some bad preconceptions with them. They may have been influenced by an event or by their peers. As a result, the Pharaoh had learnt that, to gain the support of his people for his journey, he would have to spend a lot of time communicating his vision. Support from the people of Egypt couldn't be taken for granted.

The Pharaoh also realised that, given an opportunity, everyone in the Kingdom was capable of offering something unique to the journey. He had marvelled at the ideas and input from every person involved in the test sessions.

"Some of their suggestions were brilliant," said the Pharaoh. "A woman had an inspired notion for sharpening the chisels used by the masons. Every night she used to watch her husband struggle with his tools when he got home. As soon as we gave her the opportunity to play her part on the journey, she gave us the idea. We've already tried it out and it works, and it saves half the time it took previously.

"Can you imagine what we would be capable of achieving with twenty thousand such enthused people on the journey? We could do great things."

He continued to outline the many things he had learnt to date, and they made an impressive list. He learnt that the 'Imperatives for growth' document removed cynicism, that the 'Challenges' document alleviated fears in the leadership of the kingdom and that the 'Vision' document inspired people to take part in the journey. He had also learnt that the use of all three documents resulted in a powerful demonstration of commitment from his people to the journey.

It had become clear that, on the journey, he would have to be realistic. Not everyone, he admitted, was at the same level of commitment. He noticed that his people fell into three camps: the great advocates of the journey, the supporters of the journey and the cautious. The Pharaoh recognised that it would take time to turn everyone into a great advocate.

Prem was delighted that Smendes had identified the three groups of people this early in the journey and told him that they would be covering this in more detail in stage three.

The Pharaoh also appreciated how the three documents helped his team of advisers and managers communicate the journey to the twenty teams. He noticed that many of them were already showing signs of being true leaders. There was also a consistency of message across the teams which he felt was missing previously from the journey.

"In summary, I have learnt a considerable amount in such a short space of time. I am also a committed advocate of your inscription 'You don't know what you don't know'."

Prem smiled. "You might even one day decide to change career and be a scholar!" The Pharaoh laughed.

"I'm not sure that the hairstyle would suit me," he said, under his breath.

"So far so good" continued the Sage, "let us move on to the third part of your agenda. As a result of the activities of the past few weeks and the lessons you have learnt, what new challenges do you face that we need to discuss today?"

The Pharaoh had three challenges, which he believed should be tackled as soon as possible. He explained that, even allowing for the completion of the good work by his team in the past few weeks, he couldn't escape the fact that the Pyramid was still seriously behind schedule, and that worried him considerably.

He also felt that it was time to present the 'Imperatives', 'Challenges' and 'Vision' documents to the remainder of the people within his kingdom.

Energy levels and enthusiasm had increased in virtually every team involved in the test. The Pharaoh was convinced that, by announcing the information contained in the documents, he could bring the Pyramid construction back on schedule.

He had also noticed that several members of his team were beginning to ask how the vision would be achieved. They believed in the sentiment behind it, but felt that the detail of its delivery was missing.

Prem acknowledged the three challenges immediately facing the Pharaoh and proceeded to outline the next part of the process.

He explained that, for the time being, (at least the next two months) the Pyramid construction would have to remain at its current level of productivity and schedule. He understood the Pharaoh's concerns but asked him to take a long-term view on the project. He assured him that the construction would quickly catch up.

"Trust the process. It won't let you down."

Prem suggested to the Pharaoh that there was no merit in announcing the documents to the remainder of the Kingdom. Not yet anyway.

"Remember that what you have just completed is a test, no more than that. As a result, you have been able to gauge the reaction of some of your people to your first piece of work. You have also learnt a great deal about their reaction to its presentation. Now is not the time to offer it to everyone in the kingdom."

The Pharaoh looked despondent. He was a man in a hurry and he wasn't used to being kept waiting.

"Let me explain why," Prem continued. "The reason you should not announce them now is related to the third challenge you mentioned to me, the detail missing in the achievement of the vision."

He assured the Pharaoh that his team had successfully completed stage one of the journey to completing the Pyramid. His research work had resulted in the discussion and production of the 'Imperatives for growth', the 'Challenges' likely to be faced on the journey and the overall 'Vision'. He explained that laying these foundations was important to the long term success of the journey.

He had now, for the first time, produced convincing reasons for asking his people to join the journey. He had removed any future surprises by identifying the pitfalls and difficulties in advance of the completion of the journey. This would impress his people, and he had produced a compelling vision that would galvanise support from around the kingdom to the journey. The people also had a clearer indication for the first time in his reign of what the Pharaoh was trying to create.

He had assembled a capable and experienced team of advisers and managers and, as a result of the research stage, had learnt many personal lessons from the experience.

Smendes had very cleverly organised many parts of the construction operation in the background, in readiness to tackle the challenges identified by the team. He was also reminded that, very importantly, he had built a solid base on the best spot on the West bank of the Nile. Stage one of the journey was complete. Laying the foundations had taken place.

Prem told the Pharaoh that he should rejoice on its completion and handed him an inscription to reflect on. It read:

Stage one of the journey
RESEARCH

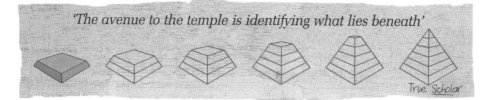

'The avenue to the temple is identifying what lies beneath'

True Scholar

THE WAY AHEAD

Stage two, which Prem called Strategy, began. This was a term familiar to the Pharaoh. He had spent many years in the company of scholars developing strategies for possible war. As a keen sportsman he had also developed strategies to win including, as a very young man, one of which he had been particularly fond.

This entailed sidling up to an opponent who had gained a significant advantage in their competition and whispering, in a voice heavy with menace, "Who's going to be Pharaoh, then?" This, invariably, resulted in a change of fortune.

Now he was about to begin the process of developing a strategy linked to the construction of his pyramid.

Prem explained to the Pharaoh that the strategy work would have nothing to do with the construction of the Pyramid. That responsibility lay with the architect and the Pharaoh's construction teams.

The strategy they would work on would be linked to the formula.

Prem had used the word 'map' several times in stage one of the journey. Stage two, he told the King, would involve its development and production. He went on to explain that the map was a manuscript discussed, developed and produced by the Pharaoh and his team of advisers.

It would be a simple document designed to announce the journey to the people of Egypt. It would include the approach that would be taken throughout the journey and would encompass the previous work carried out by the team: the 'Imperatives for Growth', the 'Challenges' and the Pharaoh's 'Vision'. It would take approximately two months to complete and would include the missing detail that the Pharaoh had referred to earlier.

Every person in the kingdom, and Egypt's trading partners, would receive a copy describing, in simple terms, the Pharaoh's journey.

The Pharaoh was, however, unhappy about revealing the contents of the 'Journey Map' and worried about it falling into wrong hands. It could be copied, and it would contain the secret formula.

Prem listened to the Pharaoh's concerns.

"Don't worry," he said. "Let me explain first of all why we need the map and then I will address your fears and concerns about its production."

"You will need the commitment of twenty thousand people to complete the Pyramid on time, I'm sure you will agree. Some are based in the quarry, some at the pyramid site. Many are by the Nile or in the desert transporting the stone, with the remainder scattered throughout your kingdom - four groups of people spread over forty-two provinces. The task of communicating your vision and obtaining the support you need will be as enormous an undertaking as the physical construction of the Pyramid"

The Pharaoh agreed.

"Consider this, if you will. With an average of one adviser, manager or supervisor to fifty people on the construction project, we have to rely on four hundred people to present the message to them. That is a huge exercise in communication. It also doesn't take into account the millions of people in the country who influence each other today, tomorrow and the next day. They also need to be involved. You can see that the map is a vital tool for us if we are to be successful on the journey."

The Pharaoh, again, agreed.

"The map, to us and the people of Egypt, will be as important a tool of support as are the sledges that transport the stone blocks or the chisels the stonemasons use. Without the map we would be unable to function."

The Pharaoh couldn't help but concur and waited patiently for Prem to address his fears and concerns.

"You are right to express concern about your enemies obtaining the map, or having it copied by others. You are also right to have concerns about the inclusion of the secrets contained in the formula, but you really have nothing to worry about.

"Let's assume for a moment that one of your enemies got a hold of the three pieces of work that you and your team have just completed. How could it possibly help them?"

Prem didn't wait for the Pharaoh's response.

"I have no intention of asking you to publish the most important part of the detail behind the work. You see, the detail I am referring to is in the hearts and minds of the people of Egypt, and that is something that can never be copied."

"The same principle applies to the formula. It is one thing to know what it is, but it is another to know how to use it. The secrets explain the process, but it's the hearts and minds of the people that make the journey happen."

The Pharaoh relaxed, as he could relate to the explanation given. He was very knowledgeable about pyramid building and matters of state, but that hadn't saved him from the predicament he was in. If the hearts and minds of the people weren't with you, you had no chance of being successful, he thought. He could also apply Prem's explanation to his team's work on stage one of the journey. If their hearts and minds had not been in the journey, they would have been unable to complete such fine work.

"Anyone can admire or even try and copy a completed piece of work" continued the Sage, "whether it's a painting, a piece of pottery or the

Pharaoh's map. But the work never reveals to the observer what has gone on in the background towards its completion. Observers have no knowledge of the pitfalls faced by the people who completed it, or the lessons that had to be learnt to obtain the end result. What often looks simple and impressive has involved many hours of pain and hard work. The secrets stay in the hearts and minds of the creators. On your journey I am referring to your people."

The Pharaoh was now a lot happier. "Remember" said Prem, "'the nut does not reveal the tree it contains'."

He asked the Pharaoh if he was happy to continue. He was, and so Prem began to explain the missing detail that was required for the map to be completed. The first thing he asked the Pharaoh to consider was what he called the 'Critical Success Factors.'

The development of these factors would provide the direction necessary to support the realisation of the Pharaoh's vision. The Pharaoh was asked to identify the main areas of focus that would have to be worked on to ensure that the journey to completion was carried out successfully. Prem gave him a few examples, such as the security of the kingdom and the availability of food and water, as a starting point.

He explained that if these two factors and others that his team would identify were not achieved, then the construction process would end in disaster and the vision would not be realised.

The Pharaoh thought this a straightforward proposition. At the palace they would often have meetings to discuss what was needed to ensure that the Pyramid would be completed. It was just a matter of pulling the information together at his next session with his team.

The second piece of work that the Pharaoh was asked to consider was linked to the behaviour of the people of Egypt. Prem asked him to discuss, agree and produce with his team what he called a culture statement. He explained that for any journey to be completed successfully, the behaviour of the people on the journey had to be appropriate to the needs of all the participants.

He gave as an example the Pharaoh's grandfather's reign, where a culture of greed, mistrust and selfishness had resulted in the Egyptian people behaving in an inappropriate manner, resulting in near disaster for the kingdom. It was the responsibility of the Pharaoh and his team of advisers to document the behaviour they would like to see demonstrated by everyone in the kingdom throughout the building of the Pyramid.

The Pharaoh remembered his mother telling him of the problems she had inherited in her early days as Pharaoh. He understood the importance of this task and looked forward to working on it with his team.

"That's all I need you to do," announced Prem. "Do you have any questions you would like to ask me before we finish today's session?"

"I have two" was the reply. "First of all, what is the best way to carry out both exercises? I am conscious of time running away with us when we get together. Also, when will we be presenting the map to the people?"

"In response to the first question" replied Prem, "ask your team to come up with the answer. It's a great test of their ability to solve the riddle of time for you. With regard to the second question, your people will receive a copy of the 'Journey Map' as part of stage three of the formula, not before. We still have a lot to do. I will meet up with you again in a few weeks' time."

The meeting ended and the next day the Pharaoh began the work with his team of officials and advisers.

Four weeks later he let Prem know that he was ready to meet again. He had completed the two tasks and was ready to present them.

When they met, the 'Critical Success Factors' were presented. These comprised eleven areas of focus that, if supported by the people within the Kingdom, would guarantee the realisation of the Pharaoh's vision. Under each factor the Pharaoh's team had included an objective to clarify what was to be achieved. They included the following:

FOOD AND WATER SUPPLY

'To provide the people of Egypt with a continuous supply of food and water'

UNIQUE EGYPTIAN CULTURE

'To maintain the unique traditions of the Egyptian culture throughout all aspects of our society'

SECURITY OF THE KINGDOM

'To maintain the security of the country against our neighbouring states and potential enemies'

FUTURE TRADE

'To increase the levels of trade enjoyed with other countries'

WEALTH AND PROSPERITY

'To ensure that the kingdom retains its status as the wealthiest nation in the world'

HEALTH AND SAFETY

'To provide the necessary resources and support required to ensure the continued well being of the Egyptian people'

LANDMARK ACHIEVEMENT

'To ensure that all agreed landmarks are achieved in the building of the Pyramid'

SUPPORT OF THE GODS

'To make every effort to worship and engage the support of our Gods'

RESOURCES

'To provide the necessary tools, equipment and resources throughout the pyramid building journey'

ATTENTION TO DETAIL

'To maintain high standards of work throughout all aspects of the pyramid construction'

TRANSPORT

'To produce routes that will enable the efficient transportation of goods and materials throughout the kingdom'

The Pharaoh then presented the second document containing the culture statements, which read:

We expect our people to:
- Play an active part in ensuring the Pharaoh's onward journey into the New World
- Understand fully the component parts of the Pharaoh's map
- Encourage and respect the contribution that others can make to the journey
- Offer ideas and suggestions on how the Pharaoh's Pyramid can be constructed successfully
- Take time out to worship and thank the Gods for their support
- Celebrate success at each stage of the Pyramid's construction
- Work hard on the journey and make the most of leisure, family and friends
- Encourage others to make a contribution to the Pharaoh's journey
- Make the necessary plans for their own journey into the New World
- Be loyal to the Pharaoh and to the Kingdom of Egypt

'Have the wisdom to abandon the values of a time that has passed and pick out the constituents of the future. An environment must be suited to an age and men to their environment'

Prem was once again impressed with the team's work and announced to the Pharaoh that stage two of the journey had successfully been completed. In what was becoming a ritual, he handed the Pharaoh an inscription. It read:

Stage two of the journey
STRATEGY

"The papyrus will negotiate the perils through the hall of two truths"

True Scholar

OBTAINING COMMITMENT

The five component parts of the 'Journey Map' had been completed and the Pharaoh and his team were naturally pleased with their achievement. Smendes was now ready to begin the process of announcing it to his people. He was in a hurry. His Pyramid was still behind schedule and he feared that his death would come before he had an opportunity to prepare for the New World, but at least he could take some comfort in the feeling that, at last, some progress was being made.

He believed that there was no need to hold the process back any longer and so assembled his scribes and asked them to produce the map in readiness. All he needed was the approval of the Sage.

He travelled to Prem's home and approached the entrance, keeping watch for lurking reptiles. The Pharaoh was expecting a short meeting and anticipated being able to proceed and communicate the map to the people of Egypt. Prem had other ideas.

He explained to the Pharaoh that, although he and his team had produced five pieces of outstanding work, there was a final component missing, and this was linked to the next use of the formula and the third stage of the journey. It was called engagement.

The Pharaoh was baffled by Prem's reluctance to communicate the map but knew that, for the time being, he would have to bow to his experience. He reminded himself that 'you don't know what you don't know'.

Prem explained to the Pharaoh the principles behind what he called the power of engagement. These principles related to all journeys and applied to the level of commitment of the people to actively play their part in their completion. He explained that, when a new journey is announced, its initial success is based on how it is communicated. People respond to the idea of the journey in different ways. They can also be divided into three distinct groups.

One group of people will support it from the outset because they believe in the Pharaoh and the purpose of the journey. They have no objections at all to being asked to commit to and support it and, as a result, will join up from day one and play their part in its completion. Prem called these people 'the great advocates' or 'the true believers'.

The second group, he explained, will do the exact opposite. They will dig their heels in and be obstructive to the reasons for the journey and their expected contribution. They often carry negative experiences from previous journeys, normally as a result of being let down. They may have experienced false or broken promises but, more usually, poor leadership. Prem gave the Pharaoh's grandfather's reign as an example of where there were many people in this group. He called these people 'the cautious', or 'the undecided'.

The third group, he continued, are caught in the middle. They are unsure whether to join the group of great advocates or perhaps join up with the cautious. They need to be convinced of the importance of the journey. They are concerned about potential difficulties in the future and how the leaders will respond. They want to play their part in the journey but they don't want to be let down by the Pharaoh and his officials. The great majority of people at the beginning of any journey are in this group. Prem called them 'the trusting', for they base their commitment to the journey on trust.

He then explained that the principles behind these three groups applied to everyone in the kingdom. The three groups had existed within his team of advisers and managers at the beginning of the journey five years ago. Three groups exist within the four hundred or so managers and supervisors across all areas of the construction project. Three groups also exist throughout the forty-two provinces in the kingdom.

The Pharaoh agreed with the groupings. He recalled noticing them within his first team of advisers and managers at the beginning of the journey. He had removed several individuals from the team and introduced new blood because of a lack of commitment and belief in the construction project. It had surprised him that some of them were so uncommitted. Now that he had heard the explanation, he understood the importance of the communication of the journey, particularly at the beginning.

Prem went on to explain that, for the journey to be successful with twenty thousand people committed to the vision, he had to first of all increase the number of leaders engaged in the journey. Twenty-five advisers and managers would not be enough to influence twenty thousand people. The Sage's plan was to develop a team of what he called 'Cultural Architects', people who would communicate with, influence and engage the people of Egypt. He explained that the more Cultural Architects there were, the more people would commit to the journey.

The Cultural Architects would initially be recruited from the first group, the great advocates, and their strategy would be to influence the middle group, the trusting, by handling their fears and concerns. Prem explained. "The level of engagement by your people will relate directly to the success you will enjoy on the journey."

He went further and stressed that a low level of engagement leads to low levels of commitment and productivity, high levels of sickness, poor time- keeping and cynicism within the kingdom. The journey will not be completed on time.

"A high level of engagement, however, leads to a high level of commitment and productivity, low levels of sickness, good time-keeping, the support of the map, including the culture statement, and, finally, the realisation of your dream; the construction of the perfect pyramid."

The Pharaoh liked the idea of having hundreds if not thousands of Cultural Architects. He could visualise the power of engagement. He could also see resistance to the title from his close friend and adviser, the architect who, like many in his profession, was a sensitive soul. He would have to handle him carefully.

"If you are happy with the principles behind engagement let's move on, as I need to explain a few other things you need to do in order to engage your people."

The Pharaoh was keen to hear more.

Prem continued to explain that one of the biggest mistakes leaders make when they want to announce a journey is to present their plans without first involving their people in the production of their map.

The Pharaoh looked at Prem in surprise, "You are not going to suggest that I involve twenty thousand people in the production of the manuscript, are you?" he asked. "It would take forever and I would be dead before we completed the exercise."

"No, I'm not, but in order for you to succeed in engaging your people, you are going to have to test again the work carried out by your team, this time in a different way and with a different group of people."

Prem explained to the Pharaoh that this test would be unlike the previous ones where they announced to the twenty teams the three documents and then gauged their reactions. This time he was asking the advisers and managers to go out to the kingdom and, as Prem put it, 'give the people a good listening to'.

"What do you mean?" asked the Pharaoh.

"Well, simply put, rather than doing what most advisers and managers do, which is to give their people a good talking to, I need you to do the exact opposite."

He explained to the Pharaoh that he needed to carry out a survey of his people's thoughts and views on himself, his team of advisers, the way in which the construction of the Pyramid was being carried out and also how the kingdom was being run. He could see the Pharaoh turning pale at his advice.

"I assume that you jest!" said the Pharaoh, "Why would I invite the people to criticise? What is the point of that?" There was a sudden and very real tension emanating from Smendes. It was clear that he still had some doubts about the value of Prem's involvement.

"Well" replied the Sage, "do you think the presentation of the map will be enough to remove the concerns and frustrations that exist in the kingdom? It might make a difference to some of the people in the trusting group, but not to the majority of them…and we could be talking about ten thousand people."

Prem continued. "If you want to survive the sting of a scorpion, you must first suck out the poison. If poison exists in the hearts and minds of the people, we need to be aware of it, and then we need to remove it. Unless you can think of an alternative way of engaging your people, then we have to carry out the survey."

The Pharaoh considered for a few moments, but he couldn't think of an alternative method. The prospect of disengaging nearly ten thousand people was too much to consider.

"As you wish," said the Pharaoh, "but how will we carry out the survey?"

Prem proceeded to outline the approach to the exercise and explained that he would personally manage the survey with the support of the Pharaoh and his team. It was considered the best way of obtaining honest feedback from the people.

In the past, Pharaohs had tried to carry out surveys themselves without using an outsider. They had always failed. Prem had learnt that, when the people are unsure of the purpose of the journey, they were unlikely to support the survey process. Only an outsider could begin the process of developing trust on any journey.

The Sage would involve three thousand people who were already participating in the current construction of the Pyramid, and a further two thousand from the forty-two provinces that made up the kingdom.

He would organise a team of one hundred Cultural Architects to meet the people and ask them for their thoughts on ten areas:

1. The overall management of the kingdom
2. The pyramid construction process
3. Each person's working environment
4. Public services, including housing
5. Health and safety
6. Communication from the palace
7. Egyptian culture
8. Support to people on the journey
9. The role of the Pharaoh
10. The role of the Pharaoh's high officials, advisers and managers

Prem produced a set of instructions for each Cultural Architect to help them to carry out the exercise. The instructions included a checklist of questions to be asked and a mechanism that could be used to filter the responses back. The whole exercise would take six weeks to complete. Prem would produce a confidential report from the feedback received and would make a presentation to the Pharaoh and his team at a pre-determined date.

Two weeks later, the Cultural Architects began the survey process with the Egyptian people. True to Prem's suggestion, they gave them 'a good listening to'. Four weeks later Prem, the Pharaoh and his team met to discuss the findings of the survey. The presentation lasted over two hours.

The summary of the findings included twenty key points for consideration:-

- The Pharaoh was hardly ever visible outside the palace. Many of the people were yet to see him in public

- The journey to build the Pyramid was viewed as a duty to the kingdom. Very few people actually wanted to take part in it

- Many people were concerned that the kingdom would revert to the bad old days of his grandfather's reign

- They were also concerned that they wouldn't have the time or energy to build their own passage to the heavens

- Anxiety existed about the security of the nation. Rumours had spread that Egypt was about to go to war with its neighbour, Syria

- High officials in the palace were viewed as remote from the people and an unnecessary expense to the kingdom

- The kingdom overall was in a worse state than when his mother had reigned

- Certain food items were unavailable at the local markets

- Regarding the pyramid construction, sledges would often need replacing, tools had very short working lives and accidents occurred on a daily basis

- Communication across the kingdom was poor, resulting in a negative, whispering 'grapevine' existing in many of the villages

- Egyptians felt compromised on several parts of their culture, which was important to them. Attention to detail and pride in their work was replaced by the need to get the job done. The perception of the people of Egypt was that the Pharaoh was in too much of a hurry to get the construction completed, at the cost of quality

- Focus of resources on the construction led to a lack elsewhere in the kingdom. There were never enough physicians to go round. Consequently, when people in the villages fell ill, epidemics quickly occurred

- Egyptians were unsure of the Pharaoh's intentions for the kingdom

- Many people felt disconnected from the nation and no longer felt proud to be Egyptian

- The people were convinced that the Gods were looking down on them and were unhappy with the Pharaoh, the people and the overall running of the kingdom

- Egyptians didn't feel recognised for their personal efforts on the journey

- Supervisors on construction sites were viewed as incapable of making decisions for themselves. They seemed to always refer back to the Pharaoh and his team, causing loss of valuable time

- It was believed that the construction of the Pyramid would never meet its agreed schedule

- A number of people believed that the Pharaoh did not make best use of the talent which existed within the kingdom

- Suggestions to improve any part of the construction were hardly ever made. Egyptians didn't believe that the Pharaoh was interested in listening to them

To support the twenty key points, Prem presented hundreds of specific pieces of anecdotal evidence reflecting the thoughts and views of the Egyptian people.

The presentation of the findings to the Pharaoh and his team of advisers ended in stunned silence. They couldn't quite believe the level of negativity in the kingdom, the lack of belief in the Pharaoh and his team, and the clear lack of commitment to the construction of the Pyramid.

The Sage asked the group what they thought of the findings. Many agreed there were no surprises in the presentation, and that they had half expected these concerns to come up, but not to the extent that they did.

The Pharaoh got extremely angry and, shouting, asked, "well why haven't you done anything to address them, and why have you allowed things to deteriorate to this level?"

The simple fact was that they had worked very hard. They had tried to manage the mood of the nation by themselves. However, the harder they tried, the worse the situation got.

One or two members of the group didn't agree with the findings of the survey at all. It didn't seem to match their experience of how they saw the Kingdom of Egypt and the construction of the Pyramid.

Prem explained to them that there was no benefit in denying the results. They had to respect the people's right to be heard and that their perception of the kingdom was their reality. For the people's perceptions to change, the Pharaoh and his team would have to change the perceptions. Disagreeing with the survey findings wouldn't get them anywhere and wouldn't lead to changing the attitude of the population.

After much discussion, they accepted the link between perception and reality and agreed that they had a lot to do as a team to engage the people of Egypt on the journey.

The Trade Ambassador, though, had a more fundamental question to ask about the survey process. "Have we not just opened up a box full of serpents, by inviting the people to have their say in the Pharaoh's journey? Surely, we have made things worse by asking them to speak."

Prem disagreed and used the scorpion bite analogy, as he had done earlier.

"Do you think that at home, on the sites, with their friends and as they play, the people are not voicing their concerns and displeasure? Of course, they are. It would be naïve of us to think that they are not. The best thing that you have ever done is to carry out this exercise," he said.

"But how" asked the Chief Treasurer, "can you say that? I don't know about everyone else in the room, but I have never felt so depressed in my life as I do at this moment."

The Pharaoh then spoke. "Is it not better to find out now and be in a position to do something about, it rather than delude ourselves into thinking that everything is well? Let's face facts, we are two years behind schedule and, if the feedback from a few thousand people on a survey is replicated across the kingdom, it's probably no surprise that we are so far behind. It's what we do with this information now that counts."

The team looked at the Pharaoh and there were nods of agreement. Prem sensed that it was time to raise the mood of the meeting. "I can see that many of you are despondent, but you should be congratulated for your courage in carrying out this work. Remember, you and your Pharaoh have carried out this exercise for the first time in his reign.

"Giving the people an opportunity to speak requires a certain type of courage. You have all just demonstrated the mark of great leaders, the ability to truly involve your people in the journey. This has been achieved by the survey process."

The team thought about it for a few moments and began to feel some optimism. One or two even smiled at their sense of achievement.

The Sage then began to explain that the 'Journey Map' could not be presented without the involvement of the people in the survey. By excluding their input, it would have been perceived as a manuscript produced by scholars for scholars.

They could now demonstrate to the people of Egypt that they had involved them in the journey development process. They had also received thousands of pieces of information, which they could now use to test the validity and accuracy of the map.

Prem told the team that, if the final manuscript addressed the concerns, fears and ambitions of the people, then the 'Journey Map' was complete, and could be announced to the nation. In effect, what the people had done was to provide the checking mechanism for the journey.

When the team heard this they were delighted with their decision to conduct the survey.

Prem then tasked the team with cross-referencing the survey results with the contents of the 'Journey Map'. He asked them to critically analyse the manuscript, to amend it where appropriate and to make it more relevant to the journey and the people's expectations. He also asked them to consider the following twelve questions.

1. Have we taken into account the needs of the Pharaoh?
2. Have we taken into account the needs of the high officials and leaders?

3. Have we taken into account the needs of the people?
4. Is the manuscript simple enough for everyone to understand?
5. Is the vision compelling enough for people to be inspired by it?
6. Are the reasons for embarking on the journey clear enough?
7. Have we explained how the vision will be achieved?
8. Are we able to demonstrate what each person's contribution to the journey will be?
9. Is the size of the opportunity communicated in sufficient detail?
10. Is it a manuscript that we would be proud to present?
11. Will it help the Cultural Architects answer any questions from other people?
12. Will it engage the people of Egypt on the journey?

If they could answer 'yes' to all twelve questions then the 'Journey Map' would be ready for presentation to the people of Egypt. Prem left them for the remainder of the day to complete the exercise. He rejoined them in the evening to be informed that the manuscript was ready.

Led by the Pharaoh's team, the nominated Cultural Architects could now introduce the map to the people of Egypt, 'cascading' it, as the Sage had put it.

Two months later, the process was complete. Everyone in the kingdom had heard about the contents of the map and had received a personal copy. Special copies were put on display throughout the villages and cities. Scholars ensured that it formed part of the school teachings for all Egyptian children. Everyone in the kingdom was made aware of the Pharaoh's journey and the importance of the 'Journey Map'.

Feedback was immediate and beyond the Pharaoh's wildest dreams. The people of Egypt were delighted with the map and detail describing the Pharaoh's journey and wanted to play their part in its completion. It was the talk of every city, village and town.

As agreed, the Pharaoh met up with Prem to give him a progress report on the 'cascading' process. They were both delighted in the way in which the Cultural Architects had played their part. After they covered the progress up-date, Prem, as usual, asked the Pharaoh what he had learnt from the 'Engagement' stage of the formula.

"I've learnt more than anything the power of engagement and the link with what I hope will be the success of the journey," said the Pharaoh. "If the people aren't engaged then we will never realise the vision. I have also learnt that engagement can only begin if you involve the people in the journey, trust them to give you feedback and then use it to support the production of the 'Journey Map'." Prem agreed.

"The map was a good manuscript before we completed the survey" said the Pharaoh, "but when we used the survey information to amend and enrich it, it became a very impressive working document. It also improved the confidence of my officials and advisers. We all knew that we had produced something that had involved the people, and that fact alone made a big difference to the team."

"What about your team?" asked Prem. "What have you learnt about them in the past few months?"

"I learnt, initially, that they fell into the three groups you described to me a few months ago. Some of them clearly weren't engaged on the journey. They didn't believe in it and, as a result, were unable to lead and influence others. The power of engagement applies to everyone in the kingdom, whatever strand of society they belong to," replied the Pharaoh.

The Pharaoh then detailed his observations on how his team had handled the 'cascade' of the 'Journey Map'. He recognised the widely differing styles and approaches across the team. He had noticed the same with the Cultural Architects. He told Prem of one specific observation he had made. "If you don't understand the map, you can't then communicate it effectively to others. If you can't communicate it to others then it's because you are not referring to it yourself. If you are not referring to it, then it's unlikely that you believe in it. Understanding and believing in its contents are critical to leading others."

Prem was delighted that the Pharaoh had made this observation. Belief in the contents of the map was indeed critical to leading others. It also reflected the frequency of its use. He explained that, in time, Smendes would notice that the people who believed in the contents of the map tended to conduct themselves in a totally different way from others. They appeared more confident and more focused on the journey and they easily overcame obstacles put in their path. Their language was often different and they would regularly make reference to specific sections and phrases in the journey map.

The Pharaoh agreed. He had already noticed that the great advocates on the journey demonstrated many of these traits and behaviours.

The Pharaoh also explained that he had learnt that, to the people of Egypt, the map represented a symbol of confidence in the journey. The symbol became more important the further the people were from the capital and the Pharaoh's Palace. He had learnt that, in the remote corners of the kingdom, the map was even more important in engaging his people as they had less contact with officials, advisers or managers of the journey. He was also more reliant on the Cultural Architects to play their part in increasing the number of great advocates who would galvanise the support of the trusting who, in turn, would try to engage the cautious.

"The power of engagement," said the Pharaoh, "lies in developing a nucleus of people who support the journey, using them to engage others. The great advocates of the journey are often not our managers or advisers, but normal people around the kingdom." The Sage agreed; engaging twenty thousand people to realise the Pharaoh's vision would require much more than the leadership of one or two high officials.

The Pharaoh finished by explaining to Prem that his current challenges involved the sustaining of the engagement process of the people and turning that into productivity on the construction of the Pyramid. The Sage agreed. It was time to reap the benefits of the hard work of stage one - research, stage two - strategy and stage three - engagement.

Before he left the meeting, the Pharaoh asked Prem what he would have to do next.

"That's easy. Make sure your officials fully understand every page of the map. Ensure also that they hold regular sessions with their people to re-affirm the contents. Support the Cultural Architects. Remember, they are your great advocates and influencers of others. And last of all, remember to keep giving your people a good listening to."

"When will I meet up with you again?" asked the Pharaoh.

"I don't know," was the reply, "you have a lot to do. You will know when the time is right. What I do know is that the power of engagement is about to put your pyramid back on schedule."

"Well" said Smendes, almost to himself," let us thank it, and the Gods, for that."

Over the next few years the pyramid construction took on a life of its own. The people were truly engaged and the productivity reached a level never previously achieved.

The Cultural Architects played their part in supporting and communicating the Pharaoh's vision and, within two years, the pyramid construction had caught up to the schedule. Within five years it had gone far ahead and it was estimated that the Pyramid would be completed in less than eighteen years. The hearts and minds of the people were very much on the journey. It was once again a great time to be an Egyptian and an even greater time to be Pharaoh.

Every part of the construction process operated impressively. At the quarry, the stonemasons carried out their work with a vigour and accuracy never previously attained, although the odd thumb still suffered an occasional bruise.

The transport team manoeuvred massive quantities of stone every day up the Nile by barge, or over the desert by sledge to the pyramid site. At the site, they had doubled the rate of work and, over five years, built nearly fifty levels of stone. The Pyramid, for the first time on the journey, was really beginning to look like the monument it was intended to be.

Everything about the construction went according to plan. The annual floods brought extra people onto the journey, including the farmers, who all supported the Pharaoh's dream. Egypt was at peace with its neighbours and, once again, the army offered their support in the quarry, in the desert and by the banks of the Nile.

The people themselves believed in what they were doing and, for the first time in his reign, supported the Pharaoh unconditionally. Food, drink and clothing were in regular supply, firewood was available and everyone in the kingdom was happy and content.

Word soon spread to other countries of the vision of the perfect pyramid. As a result, men and women came from afar to play their part in the Pharaoh's journey.

The power of engagement had achieved the effect on the journey that the Sage had promised.

Stage three of the journey
ENGAGEMENT

'Earn commitment and you will steer them on the journey to the promised land'

True Scholar

CREATING A CLIMATE OF PERFORMANCE

The Pharaoh was now ten years into the journey and the Pyramid was more than half way to completion. The architect and his team had reported that, at the current work rate, the Pyramid would be completed in seventeen years, three ahead of schedule.

The Pharaoh was delighted with the news. After the trials and tribulations of the early days of the journey, he was finally in a position where he could rely on his team to lead the journey. He held regular meetings with them to discuss all aspects of the construction. They were using the 'Journey Map' to keep the people focused on the overall vision.

The culture statement focused people on the behaviours required across the kingdom and new people were joining the journey each day. Everyone in Egypt was playing his or her part. The issues raised in the survey had long since been tackled and all reports indicated that the mood of the nation had never been better. The Pharaoh was rightly proud of his team, and of the contribution of his people. The team members were also working well. They had grown considerably more confident over the years of the journey. Even the scholars who, at the beginning, had resented the involvement of the Sage were forced to admit that introducing him had been a masterstroke by the Pharaoh.

Many commented that it was the mark of a great Pharaoh to bring an outsider into the national project.

As construction picked up pace and met the planned schedules, the Pharaoh had less and less contact with Prem. When the pyramid building project went ahead of schedule the Pharaoh decided there was no need to involve him further. The architect had predicted a seventeen-year completion period, and this had been achieved as a result of the energy, commitment and enthusiasm of the Pharaoh's team of advisers and his people. It was just a matter of continuing the journey.

Smendes believed that he had personally devoted enough energy to the project and felt it was time to broaden his horizons and learn more about the world in which he lived.

He would often listen with great interest to the stories told by the Trade Ambassador on his return from his foreign visits, usually in a new chariot. It was time, he thought, to accompany the Ambassador on his next journey and to experience life outside the kingdom. His mother would often tell him, before she departed for the New World, that he should see as much of the Old World as possible.

He announced that he would be taking a year out of the country.

He asked his team to contact him if they had any problems they couldn't handle. He assured them that they had his full confidence in managing the kingdom and continuing the pyramid building journey. As he set off he looked over at the pyramid construction taking shape, and looked forward to viewing its progress when he returned.

A year later, he returned laden with riches, full of experience, full of hope and with a greater insight into contemporary chariot design than he would have believed possible.

He had enjoyed the most wonderful experience he could have imagined and had learnt a lot about other countries, their cultures, their expertise and their plans. He intended to use the knowledge and experience gained to make Egypt an even more prosperous and advanced nation than it was at that moment.

On his return journey, his thoughts were preoccupied with the progress of the Pyramid. It was ten months since he had heard anything from his team. He assumed that all was well in the kingdom and that the

Pyramid was continuing to progress towards its completion.

From a distance, although he could see its shape on the horizon, it was difficult to gauge the Pyramid's size. As he got nearer to the capital, he could see that all was not well. He realised that the Pyramid hadn't increased significantly in height. This surprised him as the further the structure progressed, the less stone was required and each block would be smaller and lighter in weight.

The architect had told him that, once the bottom third of the Pyramid was completed, then the physical progress would be obvious, virtually on a quarter by quarter basis. The Pharaoh had been away for over a year. He expected to see more development.

He also noticed that, although the people were obviously busy, the atmosphere was different. He assumed that something significant, perhaps an epidemic, had happened while he was away. There couldn't, he thought, be any other reason or explanation for the obvious lack of progress.

He called a meeting of his officials and advisers to shed some light on the lack of progress. His team had not looked forward to his return; they knew that progress had not been good. They also knew that they didn't have the reasons why. They were doing what they had always done and were confused about the situation. It was as if they had reached a plateau on their journey.

The Pharaoh discussed the events over the twelve-month period at great length. Everything seemed to be in place, but the architect told the Pharaoh that, if corrective action wasn't taken, the Pyramid would never meet its twenty-year completion date. The Pharaoh began to think again about the prospect of failure. There was no use in panicking and, although he hadn't had any contact with Prem for a while, it was time to pay him a visit. He would have the answer, thought the Pharaoh.

The Sage was delighted to meet the Pharaoh again. He had heard about the integration of the map into the kingdom and the success the

Pharaoh had enjoyed in getting the pyramid construction ahead of schedule. He wasn't, however, surprised to hear about the plateau the Pharaoh was now experiencing. It was time to introduce the Pharaoh to stage four of the formula, what he called motivation.

Before he started to explain the fourth stage, Prem asked Smendes if he had had any thoughts or reasons why they might be stuck on what the Pharaoh called the plateau.

Once more Smendes felt himself experiencing doubts about the man, despite his obvious contribution so far. It seemed, again, that he was getting more questions when what he really wanted were answers.

Setting aside these doubts with a considerable effort of will, the Pharaoh listed several possibilities, the first one being that he shouldn't have gone away on his trip. His lack of visibility had resulted in a loss of focus on the construction project.

Perhaps he had to be constantly on site, maintaining productivity and communicating with the workforce. It could also be, the Pharaoh thought, that his team was not as good as he imagined they were. He also questioned the 'Journey Map'; perhaps it wasn't as fine a piece of work as he had thought.

"I assumed," said the Pharaoh, "that the 'Journey Map' would solve all our problems; we had put enough work into it as a team. We carried out the people survey at your insistence, we listened to the people and, based on their feedback, improved on the areas covered in the survey. There was nothing more that I could have done personally to support the journey. To say that I am disappointed with where we are today is an understatement!"

Prem explained to the Pharaoh that one of the marks of a great leader is his or her ability to leave others to get on with the journey.

"Successful Pharaohs in the past" he explained, "including your mother, went on to carry out other important duties, and yet completed their pyramids on time. You were right to travel abroad with your ambassador. The knowledge and experience that you have gained will stand you in good stead for many years to come. I can guarantee that."

The Pharaoh listened but couldn't agree with this thinking. He was too concerned about his pyramid. Prem continued. "Don't blame the map either," he said. "A good manuscript doesn't become a bad manuscript overnight. There are other reasons why your progress has reached a plateau and it's time for us to discuss this as stage four of the journey."

The Pharaoh waited for the answer to the current situation. Prem explained that it was time to carry out another survey, although this would be a survey with a difference; it would involve only the two of them.

They spent a week visiting selected villages and cities around the capital to find out where the problems lay. They both travelled in disguise and, to the casual observer, looked like ordinary Egyptians going about their day-to-day business. No one knew that they were in the presence of the ruler of the kingdom. Not even the court officials had been made aware of Prem's plan.

Both men merged into the village life, in the deserts and near to the banks of the Nile, with ease. They listened to the farmers and craftsmen, ordinary men and women and even to the children.

They visited local meeting places such as the 'Anubis and Ibis', a hostelry name that has survived to this day, much modified, as the 'Dog and Duck'.

They uncovered a staggering picture of what life was like on the Pharaoh's pyramid journey. When they finally arrived back at the Royal Palace, they spent a further two days discussing their findings and then producing, with the help of the Pharaoh's scribes, a detailed summary of life in the kingdom.

The summary included the following points:

- The map had successfully played its part in announcing the Pharaoh's journey to the people of Egypt

- Everyone in the kingdom still had a copy but very few people made reference to it

- Officials, managers and advisers in the kingdom had stopped using it or referring to it between themselves and with their teams

- New people joining the journey were given a copy and were expected to understand it. Very rarely was it explained to them in detail

- Although the people knew what the Pharaoh's vision was, they lacked focus on the journey. Many of them, through inefficiency, ended up being busy fools

- The improvements that the Pharaoh had made, as a result of the previous survey with the people, had been forgotten by the majority of the population. New problems were occurring on a daily basis and were not addressed by managers and advisers

- There was a massive increase in scorpion stings, snakebites and job-related injuries. People didn't have the same access to a physician that they were used to and, when they did, the physicians complained about the lack of juniper berries. They were unable to produce most of their fever-reducing potions

- Garlic had also been in short supply. Village magicians were also unable to support the physicians and help the people

- The people were tired. They were promised ten days' work and one day of rest, but this very rarely happened

- Consequently, they were unable to spend time with their families, time building their own tombs or worshipping the Gods

- Success on the journey was no longer celebrated as it was in the early days. It was now taken for granted by managers. They no longer saw the need to celebrate with their people

- On the sites, tools were not sharpened and returned quickly enough, sledges would often break and accidents were now happening on a daily basis on the pyramid site

- Wives and partners were unhappy because their husbands and partners were unhappy

- There wasn't as much fun on the journey as there had been

- The journey had become too serious. Destination became the priority once again. Many of the old bad habits had resurfaced

- Sickness was up, particularly on a Monday. Hangovers from Sunday evenings became part of the new construction culture

- The Egyptian people believed that the journey would be completed, but the sense of urgency and passion had waned

- Many of the people were also asked to work on the unlucky 'red' days on the Egyptian calendar

- There were great inconsistencies relating to overall morale. People in the quarry felt undervalued and unrecognised for their efforts, the transport team felt ignored, whilst the people on the pyramid site appeared to get more rewards than others. The support people in the kingdom felt they were being taken for granted. A culture of arrogance and self-importance had crept into some of the teams. Some groups started to resent others

- The people very rarely knew how the journey was progressing. The public events that they had enjoyed before had stopped. The reasons given were that the Pharaoh was too busy looking at new opportunities for the kingdom

When the scribes had completed the summary of the findings of their visits, the Pharaoh asked the Sage how to make sense of it all. The people were clearly unhappy again.

Prem replied "it's time to consider stage four of the formula and study the importance placed on motivation."

He explained to the Pharaoh that he had reached a critical stage in the journey. The foundations had been laid, the plans had been announced, the people had been engaged and the culmination was that progress had been spectacular. He also suggested that it was impossible to sustain this for one single and very important reason.

"If you always do what you always did you will always get what you always got. It is now time for a new approach to the journey. Using the information contained in the map, it is time to create a climate of performance throughout the kingdom."

He started to explain that, contrary to their findings, the people were happy and content. They had a sense of purpose in their lives; the pyramid building journey. The country was in good shape; food and water was in plentiful supply; their children were better educated than they had ever been and people were more informed within their communities. They had a lot to be happy about.

"How can you say that?" asked the Pharaoh. "Look at the response we obtained on our visits, it's terrible!"

"It's not terrible at all" Prem replied, "it's indicative of a group of people who have a higher expectation of themselves, their neighbours, their co-workers, their Pharaoh and their kingdom. They have moved on as individuals. They have learnt more and experienced more. They are no longer prepared to accept second best from anyone on your journey."

Prem continued to explain the principles of what he knew as motivation. Many leading scholars agreed that the definition of motivation was 'an internal driving force within an individual'. Every person in the kingdom had a driving force, a will to act in some way. Productivity on the pyramid construction and people's support on the journey consisted of the combined internal driving forces of each person. High productivity resulted from a high driving force and low productivity from the opposite.

The Pharaoh then learnt that, contrary to popular belief, it was impossible for one person to motivate another. All that he, as Pharaoh, could do was create the right climate where an individual's internal driving force could excel. He had successfully created such a climate when he involved the people in the contents of the map. This had the desired effect of combining the internal driving forces of his people to bring the construction of the Pyramid back on schedule.

Prem explained that stage four was about applying this simple principle throughout the kingdom and creating a climate of performance, where the people would be so motivated that their contribution would far exceed anything that had gone before.

The Sage smiled reassuringly. "This is what I am asking you and your team to remember. The time to motivate your people is when they are already motivated."

He then explained what this meant.

There were four factors that would have to be taken into account and which would contribute to creating a climate of performance within the kingdom.

1. Understanding motivation and the impact on personal performance
2. The four principles of outstanding performance
3. Personal contribution and commitment to each critical success factor
4. The need to produce a motivation plan for each team

He explained to the Pharaoh that, in order to create a climate of performance, he had first to remove any barriers that could get in the way of affecting the internal driving force of his people.

He highlighted the feedback obtained from the initial survey carried out in stage three of the journey, and from the secret visits made by both of them to the villages and cities, as examples of what he meant.

He also told the Pharaoh that there was a unique paradox in how the survey findings were handled. If ignored they would affect productivity greatly but, taken care of, they would help increase productivity initially before a plateau of performance would be achieved.

Motivation, he told the Pharaoh, was as simple as the definition and as complex as the process itself, but understanding it, he explained, would help him be successful on stage four of the journey.

"To help you and your team monitor the motivation level of your people, I have produced this list for you, which highlights the twenty-five most important motivation factors which affect performance. Use this checklist to monitor the motivation level within your teams. Most of the reasons why you are currently on the plateau are on this list. Most of our findings from our secret visits are also there. When you have the information take corrective action. This will make a difference to morale in your kingdom "

THE REAL WORLD
People Motivation Factors

Clarity of the Vision

The strength of the 'grapevine'

Involvement level in the journey

Reward and recognition

Opportunity to issue feedback

Public events and social gatherings

General visibility of the leaders

The perception of the Pharaoh

Communication of the journey progress

The setting of realistic goals

Support by managers to others

Benefits to the people

Leaders 'leading by example'

Size of the opportunity

How 'good news' and 'bad news' is communicated

Reference to the journey map

Sense of achievement

Contribution and support to the journey from others

Quality of the work environment

Influence of others throughout the journey

Opportunities available for advancement

Training and development of the people

Relevance of each person's contribution to the journey

Support to the Egyptian Culture

Level of fun on the journey

Creating a Climate of Performance

Achievement   Recognition   Participation   Growth

Prem then talked about outstanding performance and the four key principles involved that would enable the Pharaoh to create a climate of performance.

- Principle of Achievement
- Principle of Recognition
- Principle of Participation
- Principle of Growth

He explained that, used collectively or individually, they were key to meeting the higher expectations of his people on the pyramid building journey. The longer his people were on the journey, the more important these principles would be.

He then explained each principle.

The Principle of Achievement would mean his people would require new goals, targets and journey markers to be set. They would quickly become bored of hitting the same target; the journey would not be challenging enough for them. They would also become disillusioned with many aspects of it. As a result, they will look elsewhere to satisfy their hunger for new challenges in the future.

With regard to the Principle of Recognition, his people would demand new and innovative forms of reward for their efforts on the journey. They would no longer be inspired to break new boundaries on behalf of the Pharaoh if they continued to receive the same 'thank you' response from him. The key to meeting their recognition requirements was to involve others: friends, families, colleagues, officials and perhaps even other countries. Traditional forms of recognition, such as an extra jar of wine, would not satisfy their needs. Also, the more public the recognition, the more likely the Pharaoh and his team would be able to take the construction to the next level.

In relation to the Principle of Participation, Prem reminded the Pharaoh of the impact the people survey and the map 'cascade' sessions had on the journey's early success. Like the previous two principles, new and more innovative methods would be required to appeal to the people's participation needs. They would need to be even more involved if they were to support him on the next stage of the journey.

Finally he talked about the Principle of Growth. This was the principle most often neglected in stage four of the journey. He went on to explain that, as people learnt more about the Pharaoh, the journey and the kingdom, they would develop an unbelievable thirst to grow and learn even more. Growth would become a critical part of the public meetings they would organise in the future. Growth would form part of the people's expectation each time they heard more news of the journey. If their need for growth was not satisfied at a personal and work-based level, many of the people would feel unfulfilled. Eventually, this would be reflected in their productivity on the journey.

The Pharaoh listened attentively to the points made and could relate to the four principles, based on his own experience when he was very much younger. "I remember that some of the best times I had when I was a child were when I was set a target and I achieved it, receiving public praise from my family. Often, it was when I was involved in the creation of something or when I learnt a new skill for the first time.

"The four principles that you speak of - Achievement, Recognition, Participation and Growth - combined to make me excel. I just never knew that the principles existed. I always knew what inspired me to do more, and what discouraged me, but I now understand that, for me, the four principles helped to create a climate of performance."

Prem nodded at the example given by the Pharaoh.

"Applying each of them in a practical and relevant manner will be key to leaving the plateau, and achieving success on the next stage of the journey," said the Sage. He continued. "The principles also relate directly to the third factor I mentioned earlier, namely the personal contribution and commitment to each critical success factor. Let me show you how the map can be used to take your people to a higher level of performance."

The Pharaoh's eyes sparkled.

Prem asked him to refer to the 'Critical Success Factors' section of the 'Journey Map'. He then explained to the Pharaoh that one of the biggest challenges he faced was to get everyone in the kingdom to contribute on a personal level to the contents of the map. The Pharaoh agreed. He was often told by sections of his people that the critical success factors applied to advisers and managers only. Some even believed that they were the sole responsibility of the Pharaoh. Prem was about to dispel the people's theory.

He asked the Pharaoh to choose any one of the critical success factors for the purpose of the discussion. The Pharaoh chose the tools, equipment and resources factor, 'to provide the necessary tools, equipment and resources throughout the pyramid construction'.

"Who is responsible for the achievement of this objective?"

"That's easy," replied the Pharaoh, "it's the Operations Director."

"Who else has a part to play in the achievement of this objective?"

"Probably the Quarry Manager and one or two other people."

"Is that all?" asked Prem. "There must be more."

And then realisation dawned. When the Pharaoh thought about it, he realised that there were thousands of people who contributed to the achievement of the objective linked to the 'Critical Success Factor'. The contributors ranged from the labourers in the forests who supplied the wood, the carpenters who shaped the tools, the craftsmen who supplied the stone flints and copper blades. They also included the women who bound the tools together, the boys who cleaned them, the transport teams who delivered them, the storage people who kept them safe and secure and finally the supervisors who distributed them. Thousands of people contribute to provide the necessary tools, equipment and resources throughout the construction.

The Pharaoh summarised this thought. "We are only as strong as the weakest link in the chain. If any of these people fail to play their part, then the journey is affected. I now understand the part that each person can play."

For the next few hours they discussed each critical success factor. Whether it was the supply of food and water, the security of the kingdom or the health and safety of the nation, the Pharaoh realised that, in every instance, many more people could play a part in supporting each factor.

He also realised that he had fallen into the trap of thinking that it was the trade people's responsibility alone to achieve the future trade 'Critical Success Factor' and the treasury people's responsibility alone to achieve the wealth and prosperity 'Critical Success Factor'. The majority of people in the kingdom could, in fact, participate in and support the majority of the 'Critical Success Factors'. He also realised the importance of what he had said earlier about chains and weak links.

"If you can get everyone in the kingdom to list the behaviours and activity that they can bring to each 'Critical Success Factor', and then ask them to commit to supporting them on the journey, the vision - the end result - will be achieved a lot quicker," Prem said.

"Consider this," he continued, "if twenty thousand people each day contribute five behaviours to the journey, one hundred thousand activities will happen that will bring you closer to your dream of the perfect pyramid. Now that is indeed impressive."

The Pharaoh agreed.

"Imagine, now, the tools that you have in your possession to help you leave the plateau. You have an understanding of how motivation can affect people's productivity. You also have a real world document linked to your journey, and you can use this to monitor morale levels with your team.

"You also know that you have to be creative in applying the four principles of outstanding performance. Build achievement, recognition, participation and growth into the management of your journey. Link these to the development of the behaviours required by your people to support the 'Critical Success Factors' in the 'Journey Map'."

Prem concluded the meeting by explaining to the Pharaoh the fourth factor of the fourth stage.

"You now have the information to produce, with your team, a motivation plan for the kingdom. Producing this plan will enable you to motivate your people when they are already motivated."

The Pharaoh thanked him for his help and told him that he would be in touch.

Stage four of the journey
MOTIVATION

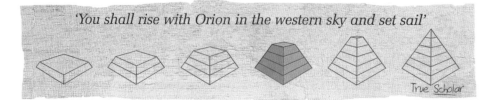

'You shall rise with Orion in the western sky and set sail'

True Scholar

MAXIMISING POTENTIAL

The Pharaoh visited Prem a few months later. "Good morning your Royal Highness" said the Sage, "I didn't expect to see you for some time."

"I have a great deal to do" replied the Pharaoh, "but I wasn't going to make the same mistake twice. I know that there are six stages to the formula. To date you've only told me about four of them. Before I put into action our work on the next stage, I thought you would discuss stages five and six with me."

"I see," said Prem with a smile. "Whose idea was that then?"

"It was the team's idea" replied the Pharaoh, "they have now truly accepted the 'you don't know, what you don't know' philosophy. They all realise that it is their responsibility to make the vision happen, but they feel that, instead of waiting to learn from the next mistake, they would rather know what needs to be done. We are ten years into the journey and an error now could cost us dearly."

"Very well, sir. I'll discuss stage five of the journey with you today but, before I do that, please give me an update on progress since last I saw you."

The Pharaoh was keen to do so for, despite his earlier misgivings, he was now really beginning to appreciate the value of the partnership he had formed with Prem.

As they strolled in the garden, the Sage's wife and daughter kept a watchful eye for anything that might approach the royal personage from the cover of the surrounding shrubbery.

The Pharaoh explained that he had held a meeting with his team to discuss the subject of motivation. He had informed them that this meant an internal driving force within each person and that it was his responsibility, and that of the team, to create the right climate where the internal driving force of each person excelled. He told them that, for the journey to go beyond its plateau, a new approach linked to motivation would need to take place.

He had also discussed with the team the many factors that could impact on whether the internal driving force of the individual was strong or not. They debated what these might be and the Pharaoh had then presented them with the findings from his and Prem's secret visits.

At first, they were shocked that they had carried out such a survey without prior consultation but, when it was explained that a further survey was required to gauge the progress that had been made on the journey, they understood the reasons why.

The Pharaoh admitted that the team were disappointed with the overall findings, as they reflected badly on their ability to manage the journey. When, however, he told them about the raised level of expectations from the people on the journey, they were able to understand and relate to this. Many of the team told Smendes, in as tactful a manner as possible, that they had a different and a higher level of expectation from him as the Pharaoh.

'If you always do what you always did, you will always get what you always got' was again discussed at great length. Although the team realised that they had achieved a considerable amount of success on the journey to date, they agreed that a different approach was now required.

The Pharaoh announced that their approach would involve creating a climate of performance. Before this could be done, the factors that might affect each person's internal driving force had to be looked at. Using the document supplied by Prem, each factor was reviewed, actions were put in place where appropriate and, in a matter of two weeks, the people knew that, once again, the Pharaoh and his team were listening to them. Corrective action had been taken.

The Pharaoh explained that they had produced a plan linked to the four principles of outstanding performance: achievement, recognition, participation and growth. These principles would form the core part of each adviser's and manager's approach to stage four of the journey. The Pharaoh handed Prem a document outlining their plan of action.

Under the 'Achievement' heading they had included five points:

- New goals and targets would be set for the next leg of the journey
- High officials, advisers and managers would demonstrate to the people of Egypt how these would be achieved
- The people would be encouraged to monitor their own performance
- Cultural Architects would support them by creating the right climate
- Additional focus on the Egyptian culture would begin removing any negative behaviour from the kingdom

A further five points were included under the 'Recognition' heading:

- People can expect to be recognised for their efforts
- A reward and recognition scheme would be produced which would involve everyone in the Kingdom of Egypt
- The scheme would be linked to the four parts of the construction process (quarry, transport, pyramid site and support in the kingdom)
- Public celebrations and events would be organised to communicate the journey's progress, achievements and recognition of individuals and teams
- Innovative rewards would be announced throughout the kingdom

The third heading was 'Participation':

- The people of Egypt would have more day-to-day involvement with the managers and advisers on the journey
- This would involve feedback sessions with the Pharaoh and his senior team
- The people would take responsibility for future surveys throughout the kingdom
- They would also take responsibility for future reward, recognition and communication events
- They would eventually take responsibility for their contribution to the development of the 'Journey Map'

When Prem came to read the section headed 'Growth', he found it blank.

"We became lost here," said the Pharaoh. "It's one of the reasons why I've come to see you. We were comfortable with the other three principles but we struggled with the fourth."

"I see," said the Sage "then I will discuss this with you in a few minutes."

The Pharaoh then told of the discussion he had with his team regarding the link between the 'Critical Success Factors' and the behaviour and activity of every one in the kingdom.

"This had a profound effect on the whole team. They realised that, although they were busy as managers and as individual units on the journey, they had fallen into the trap of working on their chosen area of function only. The Trade Ambassador had focused purely on trade, the Treasury Chief on budgets and the Operations Manager on people and logistics. They all realised, though, that we were not maximising our potential as a team. When I presented the 'one hundred thousand activities per day' example, they realised the power of the process."

Prem was delighted with the news, as this was one of the key factors to completing the journey successfully and on time. They had understood that they were only as strong as the weakest link in the chain. The Pharaoh then presented a sample of some of the motivation plans the team had produced. The plans were in their first draft, but included activity linked to ensuring that a climate of performance could be created throughout the kingdom.

The plans included more creative use of the 'Journey Map', the development of the people's working environment, public social events and gatherings, special competitions and awards, and lots of communication regarding the progress made on the journey. In each plan, Achievement, Recognition and Participation was included. Only Growth was missing.

Prem congratulated the Pharaoh on the work completed by his team. They had demonstrated an understanding of the four factors highlighted in stage four and, through the production of the motivation plans, had started the process of creating a climate of performance. It was time to explain to the Pharaoh the next part of the formula'; stage five of the journey, development.

"Stage five follows on quickly from stage four and, in some respects, has a degree of overlap, particularly with regard to the missing principle in your team's work, namely that of growth."

The Sage assured the Pharaoh that, by introducing the activity he had planned in stage four, the journey would soon move significantly ahead of schedule once again.

"Your people" he said, "will be motivated and productivity will return to its previous high level."

He went on to explain that, although engagement levels would again be strong, the Pharaoh had to be careful because accidents and unforeseen circumstances would require an additional impetus to take the journey on to its completion.

The accidents and unforeseen circumstances that Prem referred to related directly to the success of the journey. He explained to the Pharaoh that any one of a number of things could now happen.

1. The people become more productive but find the work less challenging than before
2. As a result, they look elsewhere for new challenges
3. They would be influenced by others to join up on a different journey
4. They would realise that they had grown as part of the journey and that they now had the potential for greater things
5. They might like to use their talent elsewhere
6. There will be a constant turnover of people throughout the journey. Some will leave and some will die
7. New people joining will not have the same emotional tie of others who have been on the journey from the beginning, therefore engagement can be more difficult to achieve with this group
8. If anything could go wrong, then it probably will
9. People will continue to have a higher expectation of their leaders
10. The closer to the end of the journey, the easier it is for people to lose focus

Prem explained that stage five involved preparing for every eventuality, in effect producing an even stronger structure of support.

This would involve the development of three areas:

1. Each team's contribution to the Pharaoh's journey
2. Systems and processes which would make the journey more efficient
3. Growth for everyone involved on the journey

He reminded the Pharaoh of the reaction to the vision he and his team had produced several years earlier. Smendes smiled; no other document, he believed, had produced the effect that the vision had. As a single piece of work it had truly moved mountains. People were, for the first time, aware of what the journey entailed throughout its passage. It was a magnificent document. To this day, the Pharaoh and his team of advisers and managers still marvelled at its simplicity and its effect.

He went on to suggest that it was time to transfer the lessons learnt from the Pharaoh's vision into the production of new visions, one for each operational area of the construction process. This included the quarry, transport, pyramid site and support. By developing these visions, the people would be able to connect further with the Pharaoh's vision at a more personal level by linking their operational vision to his.

This would engage people even further on the critical fifth stage of the journey.

The Pharaoh fully understood Prem's thinking, and was disappointed that the team hadn't thought of it before.

To support the completion of the four operational visions, Prem explained to the Pharaoh that the second part of the development work involved systems and processes.

"In order to produce the perfect pyramid," he said, "you will have to define what you mean by 'perfect', then produce a set of systems and processes which can be understood and supported by everyone on the journey. The scribes would be involved in their documentation and the manuscript would be discussed by the people, developed by the people and finally produced by the people."

Prem continued by telling Smendes that many of the people would be even more engaged in the journey at the thought of producing such a fine piece of work. The systems and processes manuscript would be a presentation of their pride in their work and the attention to detail required to succeed. It would also act as a reference guide should anyone be unsure of any aspect of the construction process.

"They would learn a great deal from carrying out the process, and it would satisfy their need for growth," said the Sage.

Although the Pharaoh acknowledged the thinking behind the advice, he didn't like the idea of producing a construction manual. No Pharaoh had to do so in the past, and what if it got into the wrong hands? He explained his concerns to Prem who, although he respected the Pharaoh's uneasiness with the idea, felt that the benefits on the journey would far outweigh his concerns.

"You could always ensure that the copy is kept secure and safe. On your journey from the Old World to the New World the manuscript would join you. The Pyramid would be sealed and no person would ever be able to get their hands on it."

The Pharaoh acknowledged that he had made a good point and agreed that he would discuss it with the architect and his team.

Prem then explained the third part of the development stage: growth for everyone. The Pharaoh understood its importance but, as he had indicated earlier, his team couldn't come up with five points that would help create a climate of performance.

When Prem and the Pharaoh reviewed it again, they discussed ten possible inclusions for the 'Growth' section of the 'Outstanding Performance' document:

- They could produce an education programme which would explain in detail the component parts of the Pharaoh's journey

- They could also organise refresher forums to remind people at different stages of the journey of its importance

- They could build in, as part of the previous two solutions, the relevance of the operational visions to the Pharaoh's overall vision

- Personal behaviours and activity linked to the critical success factors could also be included as part of the education process

- Cultural Architects could receive specialist training in how they could be even more effective in enlisting support from others to the journey

- Officials, including the Pharaoh's team and advisers, could learn more about leadership

- All managers could be trained in how to educate others, build teams and communicate

- Special innovation working groups could be set up to look at ways to improve efficiency across the four parts of the construction process

- Culture sessions could be organised to gauge its effectiveness throughout the kingdom

- 'Journey Map' meetings could be held to ensure it is kept up-to-date and relevant to the Pharaoh and his people

They then agreed some potential solutions. Two weeks later Smendes produced the missing five points under the heading 'Growth'. His twenty-point plan was complete.

Prem told the Pharaoh that he had finished his education relating to stage five of the journey. All the Pharaoh was asked to do was to be mindful of the link with stage four and his journey would soon be completed.

"What about stage six" asked the Pharaoh, "are you not going to explain it to me now?"

"No" replied Prem, "when the time is right I would prefer you to explain it to me. You will soon know what stage six is, and when it has been completed."

"Stage six is when the Pyramid is complete!" declared the Pharaoh.

"You decide," replied Prem, and handed the Pharaoh another inscription.

Stage five of the journey
DEVELOPMENT

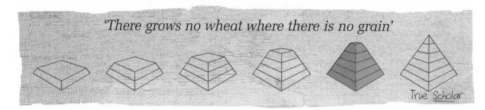

TAKING RESPONSIBILITY

Sometime later, the Pharaoh arrived at Prem's home to announce that he was ready to talk to him about stage six of the journey. He managed, yet again, to avoid the attentions of what he had come to think of as the Sage's guardian tortoise.

The Sage greeted him and was about to begin the normal structure of their meeting by asking him for an update on the progress. He would then discuss what Smendes had learnt, followed by future challenges then questions. It was a format that had worked well for both of them in the past.

This time, however, the Pharaoh had other ideas. "I'm going to take you on a tour of the kingdom. I want you to see how we are doing for yourself."

Prem was intrigued by the Pharaoh's proposal.

As they began the tour, the Pharaoh explained to Prem that he was going to witness the culmination of the previous five stages: research, strategy, engagement, motivation and development, plus the secrets of stage six of the formula.

"We have achieved a great deal since our last meeting," said the Pharaoh, "stage four and stage five have made a big difference for everyone on the journey."

They arrived at the quarry first. There was a real sense of activity and excitement. The Pharaoh introduced Prem to numerous site foremen, supervisors and people who were proud to demonstrate many parts of their work. The Sage was impressed by their attention to detail in such a physically demanding part of the construction. He looked on in amazement at the way in which thousands of people worked alongside each other and, with only hand tools, managed to carve massive pieces of stone out of the mountainside.

He noticed that the foremen had introduced competitions. Each team had a name and, at set times in the operation, the work would stop and public awards would be made. The people clapped, laughed and acknowledged the winners. Each team had a clear identity of its own and a real sense of purpose. Some of the people had dedicated their life to the journey and very clearly were enjoying the experience. From the top of the quarry, the operation looked like an ant colony.

"Isn't it magnificent?" said the Pharaoh. "A real world demonstration of confidence, certainty of purpose and synergy."

Prem could only agree.

They next visited the transport operation where the stones were moved from the quarry up the Nile or over the desert to the pyramid site.

The first thing that Prem noticed was that everyone was singing as they pulled the sledges. Again the gangs had names, an identity and a clear certainty of purpose. Competitions were once more in place.

The operation was impressive, with everyone working in tandem to ensure that no time was wasted between the quarry and the pyramid site.

"We've never moved as much stone per day on the journey as we do now. Look at the sledge operation. See how two men pour water on the bottom of the sledge. This lubricates it, enabling the stone to be carried quicker. This idea came from the people at one of our sessions in the village.

"We have several examples of such initiatives," continued the Smendes. "One of our masons realised that the harder metals used on chariot wheel hubs could be re-cast into small chisels to produce better detail work."

"For the first time," continued the Pharaoh, "the people are surprising me and my team of advisers and leaders. We explain our problems to them now, and every time they came up with the solutions…well, almost every time."

In answer to the Sage's puzzled expression, he went on. "We did have a suggestion about moving some smaller blocks of stone using trained scarab beetles. A case of too much imagination and too much sun, we thought."

They passed the gangs transporting the stone and travelled on to the Nile. The ceremonial barge that would transport the Pharaoh was near to completion, with hundreds of carpenters playing their part on what already looked like a magnificent piece of craftsmanship. Prem could see that they took great pride in their efforts. They would often stop and ask someone else to have a look at their work. Invariably, this ended with a handshake, a laugh or a pat on the back.

"What is that man doing?" asked Prem.

"He's helping us produce our manuscript which details the systems, processes and approach we should take to ensure that we maintain maximum efficiency on the journey. We decided it was a good idea. We have an official who champions it and hundreds of men and women who support the development of the manuscript. They are everywhere on the journey. And yes, before you ask, the manuscript will leave for the New World with me when it is my time to go," replied the Pharaoh.

They travelled up the Nile to visit the pyramid site. Along the banks they saw hippos and turtles, pelicans and the occasional crocodile. They also saw many settlements and, as they passed by, they could hear cheering in each village. Fishermen were filling nets and farmers were cultivating the land, everyone ensuring food was in plentiful supply.

In one of the villages, they could see women making baskets and mats. Children were carrying materials from storerooms to the working areas and donkeys were being used to carry heavier loads. In the air they could smell oxen, calves and chickens being roasted in readiness for the people coming back from their day's work. Cakes were being baked, baskets of figs and others fruits were already out on display.

"This village has just won a competition for the best improvement in production over the past three months. Tonight they will be holding their own celebration banquet. You can see how excited they are - and why not? They deserve it. Their results have been magnificent," said the Pharaoh.

Other villages along the Nile were equally busy. Cheering filled the air throughout the hour it took to sail up the river.

When they arrived at the quayside, Prem was amazed at the sheer scale of the pyramid site. The causeway leading to the Mortuary Temple had already been completed. He noticed that many officials had built tombs alongside the causeway so they could be with the King when he died.

The huge tomb by now looked like a pyramid. It was nearly three-quarters of the way to completion. The Pharaoh led the way up onto the structure. He wanted to show Prem the workmanship of his people.

"Look at this," he said. "One after another, perfect blocks, all cut and aligned with great precision. There isn't a single space between each block. Have you noticed that we never use mortar to hold the blocks together?"

Prem now knew what the Pharaoh had meant when he said he wanted to create the perfect pyramid.

"Each course is laid at a precise level," said the Pharaoh. "Look at the attention to detail on every piece of stone. See how smooth and well finished they are. Every one is a work of art in its own right."

The Pharaoh went on to explain that they had developed elite teams that they could use to identify what was required to truly excel on the construction. The lessons they had learnt were now being passed on to others. Productivity had increased, but so had quality.

"We've faced some huge challenges in the past year," said the Pharaoh.

"We couldn't work out how to move the really heavy granite blocks up the structure. Our people developed the spiral ramp concept you see surrounding the Pyramid. It was their idea, not our managers' or advisers'," he continued.

Throughout the pyramid site they witnessed leadership, teamwork and efficiency. There was a real spirit on the site. It was energising just to see it.

As they left the pyramid site to return to the palace, the Sage could see how proud the Pharaoh was of his people. He couldn't stop talking about their achievements.

He explained to Prem that understanding motivation had been important to changing the management approach of his team. Regularly reviewing the factors which affected people's internal driving force, then taking the corrective action, was also important. He had introduced the four principles - Achievement, Recognition, Participation and Growth - into the journey and they had helped in creating a climate of performance.

The workforce had also agreed to produce the systems and process manuscript, an exercise in itself, which, the people agreed, represented the quality of their work. The Pharaoh had also introduced forums, workshops, meetings and public gatherings and had again created a public sense of belonging to the journey.

Visions had been produced for the four operational areas of the construction and this had enabled the people concerned to be more focused on what was needed to support the Pharaoh's vision of the perfect pyramid.

All of this had made a difference.

At the palace, Prem was introduced to the Director of Development, who was tasked with all growth issues on the journey. She had produced education, development and leadership programmes. Everyone in the kingdom had a growth programme. She had linked each programme to the Pharaoh's 'Journey Map' and had ensured that action planning, linked to each person's personal contribution on the journey, was at the core of the programme.

Cultural Architects received specialist support. Regular public forums and meetings were held and the Director of Development was also responsible for the management of the people survey. Lastly, a career planning programme had been developed to ensure that, when people were too ill or too old to continue on the journey, new recruits would take over. The Director of Development also had a seat on the Pharaoh's royal table and had earned the respect of the officials in the palace.

Unbeknown to Prem, the Pharaoh had organised a special dinner in honour of the Sage's contribution on the journey. He had invited members of his team and other officials to the event.

As they sat and enjoyed the meal, Prem thanked the Pharaoh for the day. "It was truly impressive to witness the work," he said.

It was then that he noticed the inscription above the top table, which read:

'The man who knows how to lead one of his brothers towards what he has known may one day be saved by that very brother'.

The Sage smiled.

The Pharaoh told Prem that he could now see more clearly the journey he was on. At first, he didn't understand why the Sage had asked him to take a leap of faith in him and the process. He now knew.

He also believed that he knew the final component of his formula; the secret stage six of the journey. Prem had waited all day, and for the previous thirteen years, for this moment.

"You are eager to tell me something, sir" he said with a smile.

"Stage six of the formula is ownership," replied the Pharaoh. "It is the combination of the previous five stages with an additional twist to it."

Prem waited.

"Ownership can only ever occur as a result of involvement, creation, development and trust and I believe we have achieved this. Ownership also equates to maturity in terms of how we lead and, similarly, as everyone takes responsibility for their part on the journey. But a key twist to achieving ownership is the need to understand the link between behaviour and results."

The Sage nodded.

"For far too long we have been focusing on the end result, forgetting that it's the day-to-day behaviours from everyone in the kingdom that contribute to the successful journey. To use a sporting analogy, we were spending so much time watching the scores that we were forgetting to play the game."

Prem agreed. The Pharaoh had learnt one of the great secrets of the journey.

"Don't misunderstand me," said the Pharaoh, "we need all six stages of the formula to be successful on the journey but it's the sixth stage, ownership, that will ensure its completion." The Pharaoh then went on to talk about the other five stages.

"Stage one, research, was important in laying the foundations of the journey. The imperatives for growth, challenges and the vision helped explain the reasons for embarking on the journey; it also gave the people confidence in us as a team. They knew for the first time what we were trying to achieve.

"Strategy, stage two, enabled us to formalise the journey using the map. Including the 'Critical Success Factors and the culture statement highlighted the missing detail, our approach and the behaviours we expected from our people throughout the kingdom.

"Stage three, which focused on engagement, involved our people in the final draft of the 'Journey Map'. It also highlighted our need to listen to our people. The survey results gave a real insight into their thinking. By using our Cultural Architects, the communication of the contents of the map helped us engage our people for the first time on the journey.

"Strangely" said Smendes with a smile of recollection, "this reminded me of my mother's last words, 'great is a great one whose great ones are great'. You know I truly believe all our people are great.

"Stage four, motivation, helped us move from the plateau we were on. Again, understanding that we affect the internal driving force of our people by our behaviours and activities as a management team was very important.

"Applying the four principals - Achievement, Recognition, Participation and Growth - was also critical to moving forward. Producing the motivation plans helped us formalise our approach.

"Development, the fifth stage, enabled us to safeguard the progress made, and plan for all eventualities in the closing part of the journey. Producing the systems and processes manuscript covered us should anything have gone wrong. Without the development stage, we would have been exposed to problems at a critical part of the journey.

"Understanding the ten factors we discussed and then building them into growth was important to taking us to the next level of the journey. But to complete the journey successfully we had to understand the connection between behaviour and results. We've had to work out a list of management activities to address this."

He showed Prem his team's list:

- We need to first identify the behaviours required by the Pharaoh to be successful as the leader of the journey
- We need to identify the behaviours required by the managers and advisers
- We need to identify the behaviours required by the people

- We need to communicate the behaviours required to each person and explain how they support the achievement of our vision
- We need to remove any factors that might affect their behaviours
- We need to develop new behaviours for new parts of the journey
- We need to explain that inappropriate behaviours culminate in poor results
- We need to explain that the right behaviours ultimately produce a good result
- Managing behaviour is critical to the success of the journey
- We need to use the six stages included in the formula

"But, for behaviour to have the maximum impact, people have to take responsibility for their part in the journey, and this can only be achieved through ownership," continued the Pharaoh.

Prem looked at the list. "You are so right. The connection between ownership, behaviour and the end result is a real one. The quicker a leader can understand the link, the quicker the vision can be realised. You also have to realise that the five previous stages play an important part in the sixth stage. Without them, ownership can never be achieved."

The Pharaoh agreed.

Throughout the dinner, the Pharaoh's team toasted the contribution that the Sage had made to the journey. Even the few scholars who had viewed his involvement at the beginning of the journey as unnecessary were now converts to the formula, and the Pharaoh himself had certainly gained a very real respect for Prem and his philosophies.

At one point, the representatives of the construction crews announced that they had a presentation for the Sage.

"This" announced their spokesman, "is something that we have given great thought to, for we wanted to give you a gift both memorable and unusual. I don't imagine you have one of these!" he announced, pulling the ornate cover from a carved wooden hippopotamus.

Prem bowed to the group with a somewhat forced smile, whilst Smendes stifled what threatened to be a rather undignified guffaw.

As the evening came to a close, the Pharaoh publicly thanked Prem for his efforts and announced that he had some good news for everyone. The Pyramid would be completed by the end of the year, six years ahead of schedule.

Everyone in the room rejoiced and clapped their hands with approval. But the team had a surprise in store for the Pharaoh. The Pyramid would be completed by the end of the week.

The Pharaoh wished the Sage farewell at the end of the evening.

"We got off to a bad start, and for that I'm sorry. We've worked well together since, though, and I have learnt a great deal from you. I now understand why my mother held you in such high esteem. I would never have completed the journey without you."

"No" replied Prem. "I couldn't have completed the journey without you."

"What do you mean?" asked the Pharaoh.

"I have a favour to ask you," said Prem.

Stage six of the journey
OWNERSHIP

'Ride alone in the chariot drawn by inspiration and you will be followed by eager fanbearers'

True Scholar

A MEETING OF MINDS

At the end of the week, and to the surprise and delight of the Pharaoh and the people of Egypt, the Pyramid was completed.

It was perfect in every detail and the most magnificent monument Egypt had ever seen, seeming to reach to the very heavens. Vast amounts of stone had gone into its completion and huge numbers of people had toiled over the construction.

The limestone that flanked its sides gleamed in the sun, so much so that it was sometimes difficult to look directly at the structure. Now that the ramps and platforms needed in the building process had been removed, it was possible to appreciate just how imposing the Pyramid was, rearing from the flat desert sands as though the Gods themselves had placed it there.

It was a symbol of power, of life and of the possible.

The celebrations accompanying its completion were, to say the least, enthusiastic. People danced in the streets, strangers embraced and the takings in the 'Anubis & Ibis' were at an all time high.

To the frustration of some of Pharaoh's advisors, the country seemed to have stopped work and was concentrating on festivities, the scale of which were in keeping with the Pyramid itself.

Despite having worked with sledges and barges for many years, the transport teams were now organising races utilising their respective vehicles, although without the encumbrance of monumental stone blocks.

In the quarry there blossomed, seemingly overnight, a profusion of what would be known in centuries to come as graffiti. Some of this would continue to cause distress to citizens of a sensitive disposition for many years.

It appeared as if almost the entire population of Egypt was prepared to enjoy themselves, and celebrate their Pharaoh's achievement for many days and night to come.

The Sage, in the meanwhile, was holding his regular weekly teachings with his students. They had discussed in some detail the Pyramid and the journey. They were all aware of the six stages of the formula and had visited the site several times themselves to see the monument. They were delighted and very proud to have been part of the journey and some of the younger ones were slightly giddy with the general euphoria.

The Sage tried to turn their attention back to things academic and, in time, most settled down to their studies although, in the circumstances, the odd lapse was indulged.

They had spent most of the day discussing the 'Journey Map', including the vision. The imperatives for growth, challenges and the critical success factors were debated at length as each student challenged Prem's approach.

The culture statement was also discussed in some detail to see if it reflected the reality of the Kingdom of Egypt. All concurred.

Everyone agreed that the 'Journey Map' was a very important and almost as magnificent a piece of work as the Pyramid.

When they finished discussing the map, Prem announced that he had a surprise for them.

He opened the entrance to his office and, standing in the doorway, was the Pharaoh.

The students couldn't believe their eyes and one, at the back of the room, was sufficiently overwhelmed to give voice to an exclamation of surprise involving one of the lesser God's areas of intimate anatomy.

Prem, with due ceremony, invited Smendes into the room and explained that he had asked the Pharaoh to attend the teaching and to offer some of his experiences to the group. The students couldn't believe what they were hearing.

When they had time to settle down, and the assembled mouths could do something other than gape, one of the students asked the Pharaoh what he had learnt from the journey.

The Pharaoh thought for a few moments and answered. "I've learnt that building the Pyramid involved three different journeys running alongside each other, almost together." The students looked puzzled.

"The first journey concerned the actual construction process," he continued. "This involved the experts and the people I had around me. My team knew what they had to do to complete the monument. There was no need for me to interfere with their job function. I was very pleased that your master didn't either. He never once told us how to build the Pyramid."

The pupils laughed. They knew that this was a trademark of the Sage's approach.

"The second journey involved the use of the formula, the six stages that I know you are aware of. Without going into the details, the more we learnt, the more we understood and the more we understood the more we believed in what was possible. It was a journey of surprises, achievement, collaboration, commitment and dedication. I learnt that the use of the formula was as important as the day-to-day construction work.

"I also learnt about the power of engagement and that, more than anything, creating a sense of purpose and belonging was a key element in our success. The journey also had to be a pleasure. We spend too much time at work for it not to be enjoyable".

The young pupils could relate to that. Their teachings were always fun.

"I also learnt that the formula involved understanding the link between behaviour and results. Because of this, and the work in the six stages, we completed the perfect pyramid well ahead of schedule.

"The third journey was different, but in many ways as important a journey to take. I call it the 'journey of life' because the six stages of the formula apply to each and everyone of us."

The students sat to attention. The Sage had never mentioned to them about the journey of life.

The Pharaoh continued.

"Everyone in the kingdom, at sometime in their life, wants to build a pyramid. By that I mean they have a dream or a vision that they want to realise in the future. This will involve a journey that they will have to embark on. They, therefore, will have to do some research and identify the size of the opportunity.

"If they want to be successful, they will then have to use this information and produce a 'Journey Map'. After that they need to surround themselves with people who they trust and who can engage in the journey with them. They will then have to remain motivated, ensuring their internal driving force is high. They will also have to remove any factors that could affect their progress on the journey.

"Continuing to personally grow, by developing new skills and knowledge, will be necessary to complete the journey successfully. Finally, they must take responsibility for the achievement of their vision by identifying the behaviours needed to succeed and applying them to ensure they are successful.

"The six stages of the formula apply as much to a person's life journey as they strive to build their own pyramid as they do to the ruler of Egypt."

His words held the assembled company in rapt silence.

"Let me add this," said the Pharaoh. "At the beginning, I thought that my main concern was just about the Old World and my passage to the New World. That is, of course, still important, but so is the Real World, which is why we are here today."

The students looked at each other. One of them asked Prem, "is that why you often say that you have helped many people build many pyramids?" He nodded.

"What challenges do you now face Your Royal Highness?" asked another student.

"Only one," replied the Pharaoh. "To pass on some of your master's teachings to my son, the next Pharaoh. I won't tell him everything. I understand why my mother didn't tell me everything. Learning is often more interesting when you are living through the experience."

"What would you like to ask us sir?" asked the youngest student in the group.

The Pharaoh laughed and looked at Prem. "You have taught them well."

"Your master asked me on the day of my mother's funeral why I thought so many people attended. At the time I was surprised by the question. I have had the feeling over the years that there is something I missed. Am I right and if so, why did so many people honour her?"

Everyone looked to Prem.

"You are right. The ultimate compliment that your people can pay is to attend your funeral. It is the final component part of stage six, ownership.

"Unfortunately, you will never witness it for yourself. You will be too busy being transported to the New World. How effective you have been in stage six will be reflected by the numbers at your funeral. If ownership has been achieved, your people will be proud to say 'I helped the Pharaoh realise his vision. I helped the Pharaoh on his onward journey'. It really is the ultimate compliment your people can pay you."

The Pharaoh listened. "You are right. I suppose that the vision doesn't belong to the Pharaoh, it belongs to everyone. That is also when you realise that ownership has been achieved."

The Sage agreed.

"Although you refer to it as the formula, I understand that the real title for the six stages is the Winning [formula]. Why is it called the Winning [formula]?" asked the Pharaoh.

Prem paused for a moment before replying. "If used properly, everyone in the kingdom wins. There are no losers on the journey.

"You won because you realised your dream, the officials and advisers won because they contributed, and the people won because of their satisfaction with the completed work."

"You taught me everything I know, but you didn't teach me everything you know. What was missing?" asked the Pharaoh.

"Ah, that's for another day and another journey," replied Prem.

The Pharaoh smiled.

"Then, before I go, I have a gift for you," said the Pharaoh.

He handed Prem a document bearing the title 'The Personal Success Model'. He explained that, in the course of analysing the behaviours that were required for everyone in the kingdom to play their part in the journey, he had noticed that they fell into four categories: belief, knowledge, skill and motivation.

"This looks interesting. What does it mean?" asked the Sage.

"Ah, that's also for another day and another journey, " replied the Pharaoh.

"You will make a great scholar, " responded the Sage.

The Pharaoh smiled at the assembled class, a smile that quickly turned to an expression of pained surprise as he glanced down at his sandaled foot.

The Nile tortoise is a creature noted for its persistence.

USING THE WINNING [FORMULA]™
IN THE REAL WORLD

I hope you have enjoyed reading 'The Real World'. You will have noticed that the Winning [formula]™ is a people-based approach to growth and success. Engaging them is critical to realising your future goals and aspirations. Highlighted below are a few final points for you to consider in the real world.

- Replace your mission statement with a truly compelling vision which captures the hearts and minds of everyone connected with your organisation. Incidentally, if reading it on a sheet of paper does not inspire you, it will never inspire your people to support you. This may seem an obvious thing to say, but the number of three line visions I see that have the same effect as the outdated mission statement would surprise you. People don't understand them and they certainly don't believe in them.

- Ask yourself 'Is the opportunity big enough to make people want to change behaviour?' If it isn't, don't start the journey. Working out the imperatives for growth and linking these to your compelling vision is critical to getting off to a good start.

- Begin your journey by involving all of your people from day one. There are no benefits in working with a select group of employees in the hope that they will engage your people when the time is right.

- Begin the trust process by informing them of the challenges you face on the journey, even if it means communicating bad news. They won't thank you for any surprises later on in the process.

- Carrying out business growth surveys is critical to engaging your people. If you believe morale and trust is low at the outset, always invite an external consultant to kick start the process. Don't try to carry out the process on your own. Your people won't give you the feedback you need to move forward.

- The more Cultural Architects you have in your organisation, the quicker you will experience spectacular results. Start to identify and recruit them as early as possible.

- A performance culture is important to success. Build the achievement, recognition, participation and growth principles into all aspects of your business.

- Identify the critical success factors required to realise your vision. Use this document as the cornerstone of your strategy. Your people will be able to relate to the objectives under each factor to their job function. Watch how quickly they understand their role in your success.

- Produce your own 'Journey Map'. My clients call it a 'Blueprint for Success' or 'Plan for Growth'. Issue everyone with a copy. Ask Cultural Architects to help in the 'cascade' process.

- To be part of a successful and growing business you will need as many people as possible to enlist on the journey. The presentation of the 'Journey Map' will help you do this.

- Growth and success also implies change. Resistance can be managed by communicating the imperatives for growth and reminding your people of your vision.

- The journey won't be easy. If it were, then every business enterprise in the world would be hugely successful.

- It will involve hard work, although the number of people who wish to be part of something special never surprises me.

- It will also require careful planning. Without a route map for the journey, it is possible for participants to lose their way.

- To be successful, everyone needs to play a part. There is no room for passengers on the growth journey. Link each person's key performance indicators or goals to the critical success factors in your 'Journey Map'.

- A high level of commitment from the top is needed. Directors must lead by example. Managers must manage effectively. Cultural Architects play a very important part in keeping everyone on track.

- The business experience often resembles a roller coaster ride. There will be many twists, turns, surprises and unexpected challenges. Disappointments will test all participants on the journey.

- The journey will involve setting and passing many milestones along the way. Celebrate every success, no matter how small it may be.

- Have fun. You might not admit it, but your people spend a large ammount of their time at work. They deserve at least to enjoy it.

- A copy of 'The Real World' issued to each colleague will help describe the significance of your journey, their personal contribution and the rewards and satisfaction possible along the way.

THE JOURNEY MAP

CHALLENGES LIKELY TO BE FACED ON THE JOURNEY

- Sustaining and improving trade with other nations
- Improving productivity and efficiency throughout the pyramid construction
- Managing the Pharaoh's journey and the necessary change required
- Sustaining the Egyptian people's focus throughout the journey
- Recruiting new talent and expertise when the time was right
- Developing and promoting the benefits of the Pyramid
- Retaining existing talent within the Kingdom of Egypt
- Funding the resources required to succeed on the journey
- Developing new building systems and processes
- Communicating the journey's progress to everyone in the kingdom
- Improving the knowledge and skills of the Egyptian people
- Gaining widespread support to the Pharaoh's journey to the New World

IMPERATIVES FOR GROWTH

THE PHARAOH'S JOURNEY INTO THE AFTERLIFE
The most important reason for us embarking on the journey. Our Pharaoh is a God. Only he can represent us and ensure that our dreams and ambitions can become a reality. Helping him on his journey into the Afterlife will benefit us all.

THE PASSAGE TO HEAVEN FOR ALL EGYPTIAN PEOPLE
Linked to the 'Imperative' highlighted above, our Pharaoh will talk to the Sun God Osiris on our behalf and will ensure that when it is our time to pass onto the New World, our passage to heaven will have been prepared in advance for us.

EGYPT'S STATUS IN THE WORLD
As Egyptians we pride ourselves in our status as the wealthiest country in the world. Everyone playing his or her personal part on the Pharaoh's journey will ensure that our status will remain for generations to come.

THREATS
We know that our enemies are envious of our wealth and our success. Given an opportunity, they will attempt to steal our riches and rob us of our future. Building the Pharaoh's Pyramid will send a message out to them that we are ready and willing to defend our nation.

FUTURE WEALTH AND SECURITY
Building the Pyramid and supporting the Pharaoh on his journey will ensure future wealth and security for our people. Our children and our children's children will benefit from the Pharaoh's journey.

APPROVAL FROM THE GODS
The Sun God Osiris has a high expectation of the people of Egypt, as do many other equally important Gods. We have a duty to worship them, support our Pharaoh and maintain their approval of our wishes and dreams for our great kingdom.

THE 'VISION'

Our overall 'vision' is to create for our Pharaoh and the Kingdom of Egypt a monument, which will transport our King to the heavens above where he will meet our Sun God Osiris in the New World. Our plan is to construct the perfect pyramid. This will be a structure unlike any built beforehand in terms of design, attention to detail and overall scale. It will be a truly impressive monument and a testament to the design and construction expertise of the people of Egypt. It will also be constructed to stand throughout the ages to come.

Future generations of people in Egypt and around the world will visit the Pharaoh's tomb and will marvel and admire at the ingenuity and workmanship.

We aim to maintain the unique Egyptian cultural and construction traditions within the structure. The secrets of the Pyramid will continue to remain secret.

Every person in Egypt will play their part in its construction – at the quarry, on the pyramid site, in the deserts, the villages and by the banks of the Nile. Farmers supplying food to our people will be recognised and rewarded for their contribution to the journey as much as the craftsmen on the pyramid site or the high officials at our palaces around the kingdom.

The Pyramid will be known throughout the kingdom as a place to worship and a place at which to feel proud to be an Egyptian. On the 'Journey to Completion' our people will be supported in every way possible to ensure the Pyramid's successful and timely completion. Dedication, passion and teamwork will describe the core values of each person on the journey.

The culmination of the support by the people of Egypt will be the completion of the perfect pyramid ahead of the agreed schedule. The measurement of the nation's success will be the successful transportation of our Pharaoh from the Old World to the New World and the pride and satisfaction from each Egyptian knowing that they played their part in his onward journey.

CRITICAL SUCCESS FACTORS

1. FOOD AND WATER SUPPLY
'To provide the people of Egypt with a continuous supply of food and water'

2. UNIQUE EGYPTIAN CULTURE
'To maintain the unique traditions of the Egyptian culture throughout all aspects of our society'

3. SECURITY OF THE KINGDOM
'To maintain the security of the country against our neighbouring states and potential enemies'

4. FUTURE TRADE
'To increase the level of trade enjoyed with other countries'

5. WEALTH AND PROSPERITY
'To ensure that the kingdom retains its status as the wealthiest nation in the world'

6. HEALTH AND SAFETY
'To provide the necessary resources and support required to ensure the continued well being of the Egyptian people'

7. LANDMARK ACHIEVEMENT
'To ensure that all agreed milestones are achieved in the building of the Pyramid'

8. SUPPORT OF THE GODS
'To make every effort to worship and engage the support of our Gods'

9. RESOURCES
'To provide the necessary tools, equipment and resources throughout the pyramid building journey'

10. ATTENTION TO DETAIL
'To maintain high standards of work throughout all aspects of pyramid construction'

11. TRANSPORT
'To produce routes which will enable the efficient transportation of goods and materials throughout the kingdom'

CULTURE STATEMENT

We expect our people to:

- Play an active part in ensuring the Pharaoh's onward journey into the New World
- Understand fully the component parts of the Pharaoh's 'Map'
- Encourage and respect the contribution that others can make to the journey.
- Offer ideas and suggestions on how the Pharaoh's Pyramid can be constructed successfully
- Take time out to worship and thank the Gods for their support
- Celebrate success at each stage of the Pyramid's construction
- Work hard on the journey and make the most of leisure, family and friends
- Encourage others to make a contribution to the Pharaoh's journey
- Make the necessary plans for their own journey into the New World
- Be loyal to the Pharaoh and to the Kingdom of Egypt

THE SIX STAGES OF THE 'GROWTH' JOURNEY

1. RESEARCH
"The avenue to the temple is identifying what lies beneath"
- Imperatives for 'Growth'
- Challenges
- Compelling 'Vision'

2. STRATEGY
"The papyrus will negotiate the perils through the hall of two truths"
- Critical Success Factors
- Strategic Objectives
- Culture Statement

3. ENGAGEMENT
"Earn commitment and you will steer them on the journey to the promised land"
- People Survey
- Journey Map
- Cultural Architects

4. MOTIVATION

"You shall rise with Orion in the western sky and set sail"

- 'Snapshot' Surveys
- 'Real World' Factors
- Outstanding Performance
- Personal Contribution
- Motivation Planning

5. DEVELOPMENT

"There grows no wheat where there is no grain "

- Unforeseen Circumstances
- Team Contribution
- Systems and Procedures
- 'Growth' for everyone

6. OWNERSHIP

"Ride alone in the chariot drawn by inspiration and you will be followed by eager fanbearers"

- Behaviour and Results
- Taking Responsibility
- Journey Success

ACKNOWLEDGEMENTS

The Winning [formula]™ journey culminating in the 'The Real World' has taken fifteen years to complete. In that time, a number of people have supported, assisted and encouraged me along the way.

My grateful thanks go to the consultants who have helped shape the development of the Winning [formula]™. Professor Lawrie Wood provided expertise in research and employee survey development. John Lunt contributed valuable leadership and management development input. Richard Morley's Neuro Linguistic Programming and coaching experience proved invaluable in helping me redefine the future direction of the business.

My thanks go to every one of my clients, past and present, who have contributed enormously to my understanding of their businesses and the challenges facing them as they grow their organisations. Their honest, frank and encouraging feedback has contributed enormously to my success.

A number of people have been instrumental in supporting my business at different stages of its development. They may not have realised their influence at the time and, for this reason, I would like to take this opportunity to thank Dr Sheila Owen Jones, Richard Holt, Tom Kenny, Linda Salmon, Carol Ward, Lesley Drury, Paul Hillman, Ian Blackhurst and Lloyd East.

My special thanks go to Tim Leaman, Gary Dewhurst, Mike and Dot Stuart, Frank and Lesley Rogers and Andy Piggott for their continued friendship and support.

The business could not have been successful without the support of my colleagues. Sallie Maskrey deserves a special mention. I have yet to meet anyone with her work rate, dedication and commitment to our customers.

The Winning [formula]™ brand has enjoyed several makeovers since its inception. Kevin Steele, Rob Smith and Philip Dyer have all contributed to its development.

With regard to the completion of 'The Real World', my thanks go to Alan Bentley and his team for their design and editing input, and to Andy Pearson for his creative and editing support. My thanks also go to Patrick Cauldbeck, Nicola Bramwell, Carl Fitzsimmons and Peter O'Brien for their proof reading and impartial feedback on the draft manuscript.

I am indebted to the wisdom and encouragement of Frank Price, author of 'Right First Time' and 'Right Every Time'. Sadly, Frank is no longer with us. Before he passed away, I learnt a great deal from him on the projects we worked on together. These were great days and I miss him very much. His advice before his untimely death was 'never write a business book without humour'. I hope I have done him proud.

Finally, my thanks go to the most important person in my life, my wife Linda. She is a constant source of inspiration to me. Without her love and encouragement 'The Real World' would not have been possible.